THE BEREAVED PARENTS'
SURVIVAL GUIDE

THE BEREAVED PARENTS' SURVIVAL GUIDE

Juliet Cassuto Rothman

Continuum • New York

For my husband, Leonard, with love

1997
The Continuum Publishing Company
370 Lexington Avenue
New York, NY 10017

Printed in the United States of America

Library of Congress Cataloging-in-Publication Data

Rothman, Juliet Cassuto, 1942–
   The bereaved parents' survival guide/Juliet Cassuto Rothman.
      p.   cm.
   Includes bibliographical references.
   ISBN 0–8264–1013–8
   1. Bereavement—Psychological aspects.   2. Grief.   3. Death—Psychological
aspects.   4. Children—Death—Psychological aspects.   5. Loss (Psychology)
I. Title.
BF575.G7R69   1997   96–49880
155.9'37'085—dc21   CIP

CONTENTS

ACKNOWLEDGMENTS

I am grateful for the assistance of other bereaved parents, who patiently read this manuscript and offered suggestions and support. I especially would like to thank Ann and Noel Castiglia, parents of Tria; Marlen and Gene Maier, parents of Eric; Paula Muelhauser, mother of Chad; Joan and Carl Para, parents of Brian; Rose Queen, mother of Rashad; Donna Rohrbaugh, mother of James Ryan; and Vickie Waidner, mother of Jonathan and Chip.

My husband, Leonard, offered encouragement, understanding, and support daily, read and reread the manuscript patiently, spent many evenings alone while I worked, and helped me "birth" each chapter from my printer, often at 3 A.M. Without his help, this book could not have been written.

INTRODUCTION

On July 3rd, 1992, my husband and I received a call that changed our lives forever. Our son had been severely injured in a diving accident. He died on September 17th, 1992. Since then, we have been bereaved parents.

I felt then, and feel now, that a chasm exists between the person that I was and the person that I am. The external physical landmarks have remained the same in my world. The internal mental, physical, and emotional ones have shifted and continue to shift.

During the first months after the death of my son, the shifts were huge. They left me often adrift in unknown waters with no oars. Even if I had had oars, I would not have known in which direction to paddle. They left me abandoned on deserted islands, with no one to talk to. They left me on mountain peaks where I searched for God, the Universe, explanations, and found only silence and the echoes of my own cries. Perhaps most painful were the shifts that left me in my own world, a world in which I had become a stranger. I could not move in that world as I had always done. I did not know how to move. So, for a long, long time, I did not move. I remained locked into myself, a shell of the person that I used to be.

During those early weeks and months, I struggled to try to understand what had happened to me. I struggled with the terrible physical pain that accompanies loss. I joined a support group of other bereaved parents. I read books about the stages of grieving. I searched for anything related to losing a child that I could find. I read about life-after-death experiences and angels. I read religious tracts. I cried a lot.

After a while, another shift occurred. I went back to work and realized that a tremendous source of information and help was available to me within my own profession. I am a social worker and teach at the National Catholic School of Social Service. For years I have worked with death and dying, counseling terminally ill patients and families about life support, advance directives, and their feelings about the ends of their own or their loved ones' lives. I have worked with bereaved sons and daughters, spouses, friends. I read and reread all that I could about counseling the dying and the grief-stricken, and tried to apply those ideas and suggestions to myself.

To prepare better for working with the deep questions that surround death and dying, I had, five years before my son's death, returned to school to study philosophy. I had attempted to integrate the wisdom of the great thinkers into my own, into my work with clients, and into my teaching. When my son died, I knew that I needed some of these broader perspectives to help myself understand what had happened.

Over the years, the shifts have gotten smaller and less sudden. I have learned that I can direct and control them, sometimes. I still cry. I grieve every day, but I have learned to ride the waves a little better, and not to get "undertaken" as my children used to say, as often and as easily as I had.

I have tried to reach out to others who have experienced the terrible loss of a child. I have tried, using all of the experiences that I have had, all of my professional skills, and all of my philosophical perspective, to help others walking slowly and painfully on that sorrow-filled path. Wanting very much to help others, I have found that I help myself as I help them, that each person with whom I share experiences gives me a gift of new understanding.

I must return, again and again, to the words of the Serenity Prayer:

God help me to accept the things I cannot change

The strength to change the things I can

The wisdom to know the difference.

My child is dead. I cannot change that. Neither can you. I can change how I react to this death, how I integrate it into myself and my life experience. It is to help us all with this task, one of the hardest we will ever encounter, that this book is written.

I am honored that you will share this journey with me. We will walk this path together. I salute you and reach out my hand to you. You are my brothers and sisters.

CHAPTER ONE

THEORETICAL PERSPECTIVES

Although they are not primary to our task, theories can provide us with a framework for understanding what has happened, is in fact still happening, to us. They help us to put our own reactions and thoughts into perspective. In a way, they help us to see that we are not alone, and that others have walked this path before us.

It is only recently that work has been done in understanding the feelings, thoughts, and problems of bereaved parents specifically. The theories I will be sharing with you are based on work with loss in general. From my experience, the "stages" of grieving are reasonably true for bereaved parents as well, but our time frames are vastly different. Loss of a parent is "natural," often expected. Loss of a spouse is much more complex—the loss of a life companion affects every aspect of our beings. Yet we know from the beginning that, in all likelihood, one of us must precede the other on that journey into the unknown. Loss of a child, however, violates every concept of "the natural order of things." We scream out at this violation in fury, again and again. No amount of preparation makes letting go easy. It is unfair, unnatural, and ultimately seems completely unacceptable.

Nonetheless, there are elements which we share in common with all others who have experienced loss. We are angry, we deny, we "bargain." We seek to drown our pain in "what if's." And, hopefully, at some point we reach a place of understanding and peace.

The best known work on the subject of death, dying, and bereavement is that of Elisabeth Kübler-Ross, who has also written about death and children. A "holistic" approach, called "The Process of Grieving," was developed by John Schneider. A brief summary of these two ways of describing and understanding grieving may be helpful to you as you try to grasp where you are and where you are going. I have tried to adapt the wording of the stages of griev-

13

ing to our needs as bereaved parents, but both of these theories can apply to any loss of a loved one.

WORK OF ELISABETH KÜBLER-ROSS

Elisabeth Kübler-Ross studied death and dying over a period of many years before developing her model for the grieving process in 1969. She defines a series of five "stages" that people pass through in coping with, and understanding, death. Although she first used this model with people who were sick and dying, she then realized that families followed the same kind of pattern in trying to cope with loss of a loved one.

• Stage One: Denial and Isolation

The first time you are told that someone that you love has died, your reaction is one of denial. "Oh, no," you think, "it can't be my child. It must be a mistake."

This denial acts to protect you from the immediate overwhelming pain of your loss. You may try to avoid facing the details and isolate yourself from what has happened and the direct evidence that cannot be avoided. You may ask for medication to block the reality of the pain from reaching you and to allow you the escape of sleep.

Denial, Kübler-Ross says, is a normal, healthy first reaction to the shock of loss.

• Stage Two: Anger

As you find yourself unable to keep denying what has happened, you become angry. Your anger may be turned toward the dead person, for abandoning you, toward God, toward the world in general, toward the person "responsible," or toward those who are not suffering the loss.

Anger may also be expressed as hostility, envy, and resentment at what has happened to you. When you are in this stage, you are questioning constantly "Why me?" "Why my child?"

• Stage Three: Bargaining

As you move past some of your anger, you enter another kind of reasoning stage. This is the stage of "if only."

"If only I hadn't let her play out in the street."

"If only I had made him come right home from school."

"If only I had gotten to the doctor sooner, gotten a better doctor, gotten another consultation."

"If only I had not answered the telephone at that moment. If only it had not rung just then."

"If only God had answered my prayers."

The loss has occurred. But in your head and heart you try to rewrite the scenario, avoiding the circumstances that caused the loss.

Focusing on the "if only's" relieves us a little, if only for a while. We know that we are deluding ourselves—our child has died and there are no "if only's" possible.

• Stage Four: Depression

When we are forced to accept that the "if only's" are really no longer possible, we find ourselves feeling depressed. We recognize that this loss has occurred and that it is irreversible. The sense of despair dominates our days. We may be unable to eat and sleep normally or function in our daily activities.

This is the stage at which just getting out of bed in the morning is an incredible effort, and getting dressed seems impossible. Our movements may be slow and lethargic. We have no energy, no will, no interests. Groups of people may overwhelm us and we prefer to be alone with our grief. We are fully absorbed in our grieving.

• Stage Five: Acceptance

Though we may feel far, far away from this stage, and may, in fact, feel that it is not possible to ever reach it, there comes a time when we are weak, tired of mourning, reconciled to our loss, and accepting of what has happened. We are peaceful, resigned, and ready to move forward into life again—slowly and very tentatively.

You may find yourself moving through these stages very slowly and unevenly. You may be in stage three today, and slip back to stage two tomorrow, next week, or next month. You may feel as though you are in more than one stage at a time—you may bargain, for example, give up, be depressed, go back and bargain again.

But slowly, patiently, inexorably, you will find yourself moving forward through these stages toward an acceptance of your loss.

WORK OF JOHN SCHNEIDER

In 1984 John Schneider developed an eight-stage model of how people grieve. His work focuses on the personal growth that can occur within the loss and the grieving. His way of looking at loss includes your whole person: your body, mind, emotions, behavior, spirituality, and beliefs.

As with Kübler-Ross's stages, you will find that you are never entirely at any one stage. You will move back and forth. You may progress quite steadily for a while, then encounter an anniversary, a birthday, or other event that pushes you temporarily back to an earlier stage in the process.

• Stage One: Initial Awareness of Loss

Schneider describes our initial awareness of our loss in terms of shock, numbness, confusion, detachment, and disbelief. Our entire system feels thrown off balance, and we may feel disoriented as well.

• Stage Two: Attempts to Limit Awareness

We try to hold on, to limit our awareness of what has happened by using ways that have worked for us in the past when we have had to cope with difficult or painful events. We are trying to avoid total loss of control, feelings of helplessness, and despair. During this stage, we may feel our muscles tensing, be unable to sleep normally, feel guilty, and think about "if only." We believe we must be in control of ourselves. We look for someone, or something, to replace our loss, think about it constantly, even have periods of feeling unexplainably happy. We also feel guilty.

• Stage Three: "Letting Go"

We begin to separate from the child we have lost, recognizing that we can not hold on to the illusion that death did not happen, or that we can avoid facing it. When we let go, we may feel depressed, contemplate suicide, or feel ashamed, anxious, or cynical. We may reject the lost loved one, and may also decide to give up our beliefs, values, and ideals.

• Stage Four: Awareness of the Depth of Our Loss

During this stage, we are able to let in a real awareness of the extent of our loss. This stage is most clearly identified as "mourning"—we feel pain, helplessness, loneliness, and hopelessness. We may feel extreme grief and feel defenseless against it. The extent of our grief may make us feel exhausted. We may have pain, and feel weak and empty. We are unable to think forward into the future, and feel overwhelmed with unbearable sorrow.

• Stage Five: A New Perspective on the Loss

We find that we are at a point of acceptance—what has happened has happened, our child has died, and we must make peace with this unalterable fact. We begin to understand that we have grown through the process of grieving. We also understand the permanence of our loss. We understand and accept the extent and limit of our personal responsibility for our child's death. We also understand and accept the limits of our child's own responsibility for what has occurred.

We become more patient, accepting, and forgiving. We can fondly remember past events in our life with our child, and experience moments of peace.

• Stage Six: Resolution of Loss

We reach the point at which we have resolved the loss we have experienced when we are able to move into activities that are not connected to our loss. It is a time of facing any unresolved issues, forgiving, accepting responsibility, and, finally, letting go. We begin to care for ourselves again, forgive ourselves and others, and find peace.

• Stage Seven: Reformulation of Loss in a Growth Context

Moving toward growth through the loss involves discovering the potentials, rather than focusing on the limits, that the loss has given us. We begin to be curious again, engage fully in life, see our grief and loss experience as a challenge that we can work through. We become spontaneous, centered, and balanced, and have a sense of integrity and wholeness. We also become more aware of our senses.

• Stage Eight: Transforming Loss into New Levels of Attachment

During this final stage of the grieving process, we transform our loss into an awareness of a new level of interconnectedness and interrelationship, a wider and greater understanding of our capacity for growth. We feel whole, creative, empathetic, committed; we are aware of our greater strength. We are open to life, to experiences, to relationships, to growth.

UNDERSTANDING YOURSELF AND YOUR GRIEVING

These two models of how we grieve can only serve as potential guides to self-awareness and understanding. You may find that you are able to gain some sense of control over your grieving by being able to read ahead and explore, at least in part, some of the tasks and experiences that lie before you.

Theories can give us a framework within which we can attempt to grasp the bare outlines of the difficult process we must experience. In a broad sense, they "fit" us all. However, the manner in which we each move through this experience is different for every one of us.

Each of us grieves in a way that is uniquely our own. It is defined and molded by our personal history, beliefs, and values. It is shaped by the relationship between ourselves and our dead child, between ourselves and significant others in our lives. Be patient with yourself—you are experiencing a terrible tragedy, and a terrible loss. Give yourself time, and space, to understand it. Be kind to yourself and loving.

CHAPTER TWO

UNDERSTANDING OURSELVES

A terrible thing has happened. Our child has died. We are overwhelmed with grief, anger, and guilt. We hurt in our hearts, our bodies, and our minds. How can we begin to understand what has occurred and how we feel about it?

I believe we must begin with ourselves.

OUR PERSONAL HISTORY

We did not arrive at this moment empty of experiences. We have known other losses, other sorrows, as well as other struggles. We have known joy and happiness, triumph and despair, silence and solitude.

The person we bring with us to our loss, the individual human being that we are, matters. In the very beginning, we think little about ourselves. All of our thoughts are on the child we have lost, on the events that led up to that loss, and on the events immediately following it. We recognize our own loss in the death of the child. We do not consciously and willingly stop to think about our own lives, about the person we were at the moment that the loss occurred. And yet, if we are to survive, we must understand that person.

All of us have encountered obstacles along the paths we have walked. All of us have scars that we carry, painfully and often secretly, from our past. For some of us, these past experiences were overwhelmingly difficult.

Have you experienced emotional, physical, or sexual abuse, neglect, or abandonment? Did you have a hard time in school? With friends? Were you often without the things you needed, or thought you needed? Was life always easy for you; was this the first difficulty you have encountered? Did you succeed at most things, do well in school, get the job you wanted?

Most of us are some mixture of these two extremes—we've had some hard times, and some good times. What these were specifically, of course, is different for each of us. We surely have strong feelings about many of our life experiences, and we bring this past, this history, and these experiences with us when we face our loss. They will affect how we understand ourselves and what has happened.

For some of us, the agony of the loss blocks out all memories, at least temporarily. For others, memories of other losses come flooding back, and their pain is superimposed on the pain of the loss of our child. The losses do not have to be of the same kind: a working parent, a friendless school year, a move, parents who divorce, the loss of a job, a task failed or abandoned, often evoke pain that seems to merge with this new, overwhelming pain. We may react now as we did then. If we have experienced serious difficulties, we may find that we are unable to face the loss of our child and move through it. We may remain "stuck."

If you think this may be happening to you, you might want to consider getting professional help. Many bereaved parents find that extensive personal help and counseling is needed, for old issues must be addressed before any healing and growth can occur.

OUR PARENTING HISTORY

For many of us, most of our adult lives have been spent as parents. Caring for our children, watching and helping them to grow, worrying over their problems, and exulting in their successes was a central part of daily experience. Some of us had to leave our children every day to work, or were separated from our child by divorce, and were keenly aware of what we were missing. Some of us saw our child as ourselves in miniature—both for good and for bad. Some of us wanted our child to do and be all of the things that we were unable to accomplish. Some were angry, disappointed, frustrated, by the path our child had chosen. All of us, however, saw in our child the future, ourselves, eternity.

Each of us has a parenting history. And, being human, that history does not exemplify perfection. We have all made mistakes. Do you think you were too lax, didn't discipline enough? Do you think you should have spent more time with your child? Did you blame her for things she didn't do? Let him get away with a lie? Were you stricter than other parents about curfews? Did you lose your temper and hit your child sometimes? Did you let your child eat junk food? Make your child attend an after-school activity that he hated? Send her to day camp when she didn't want to go? Make him pay for gas to teach him responsibility? Fill the tank and find it taken for granted? Overprotect? Encourage risk? Did you minimize medical problems which needed attention? Teach your child to worry over every lump and bump?

We are our own harshest judges. And, when our child has died, the way in which we judge ourselves as parents makes us suffer all the more. Why did I make him save all his money for college, and not let him spend it on fun? He didn't even get to go! Why didn't I get her that expensive prom dress she wanted? It was her last dance! Why did I ground her for "talking back"? Maybe she was just trying to express herself! Why didn't I take time off for his school play? He'll never be in another.

In some families, a child's long and debilitating illness has drained physical, emotional, and financial resources from each person, as well as from the family as a whole. The sick child has been the focus of all family attention, and family life tended to revolve around her needs and problems. Other family members, especially children, may have felt set aside, ignored as less important. They may have been expected to make sacrifices of parental time and interest to the sick child. Parents caring for a sick child often feel guilty for the attention that they are taking from other members of the family. They are aware that others are suffering, but feel trapped by their love and care for the child most in need. This may happen, for example, when a child with AIDS, who perhaps has been out of the home for a period of time, returns home in the final stages of the disease.

The child who has died may have had severe problems which have been a source of torment to you for many years. Mental illness, substance abuse, alcoholism, abusive behavior, aggressive and violent acting-out, criminal behavior, incarceration, delinquency and truancy, and many other problems may have been a part of your child's life that you could not understand, could not accept, could not solve, no matter how hard you tried. Your child was "always in trouble," "always creating problems for everybody," "always fighting." Your life seemed to go from crisis to crisis, with no end in sight, and you felt yourself imprisoned by your relationship. You had given birth to this child, raised him as best you could, but his problems seemed to overwhelm you at every turn.

If your child has had a long illness, or consuming and seemingly unresolvable problems, you may have a feeling of relief when death occurs. The long agony, of both yourself and your child, is over. No longer must you postpone and sacrifice your own needs and those of others to devote yourself to the needs of your child. No longer must you worry and wait for the phone call that announces the next crisis, the next problem, in your child's turbulent and painful life. No longer must this child be for you a source of pain, embarrassment, and guilt. It is over, and relief is a natural feeling.

You may feel guilty for feeling this sense of relief. This, too, is natural, for it seems to us so very wrong to be relieved when we have lost a child. Be kind to yourself—both the relief and the guilt for the relief are transitory feelings. You will find that you will soon move from these feelings to a more profound reaction that is the kind of grief that you are expecting to feel.

Even if you have not had these more severe problems in your relationship with your child, you may experience difficulties as you remember, and try to deal with, some of the negative feelings that you have had for this child that you have never expressed. Perhaps you weren't comfortable with her temperament; you and she were never really in synch, and you felt that, as the parent, you should have somehow "fixed" this. Perhaps he was weak and unathletic when you had wanted a son who would play baseball just like you did; you wanted to coach the Little League and he disappointed you. Perhaps he looked like Uncle Willy, and you always disliked Uncle Willy and thought he was a jerk. Perhaps she was big and awkward, and you were petite and you felt secretly embarrassed that she was your daughter. Or he always gave you an argument about everything and never just did what you told him to do and you sometimes wanted to avoid him. These things are on a list so secret we don't even want to look at it ourselves. We all have lists of things like these, ones we can talk about easily, and ones we can't.

We can go on and on with our lists. All parents can. Only they still have time to repair the damage, and we do not.

And yet, we must forgive ourselves.

OUR SELF-IMAGE

Personal histories and parenting histories contribute to the way we think about ourselves, to our self-image. I do not think that too many people think of themselves as perfect. We all see our defects, and these make us vulnerable. This is true of everybody—all of us, bereaved or not.

Low self-esteem can come from a number of sources. Some of these come out of our personal histories, things we have experienced growing up. Some are our own impressions of ourselves. Many of us are not happy with our appearance or our accomplishments. We're too fat or thin, too tall or short; our hair is curly or too straight or falling out. We are not as smart, not as educated, as we would like to be, and we do not have the jobs and careers that we wanted. We do not provide for our families all of the things that they want and need. We are not artistic, can't sing on key, are poor spellers, are unathletic. The list of possibilities is endless.

When bad things happen to us, we often look to ourselves for the reasons. I'm not popular because I'm overweight. They think I'm a nerd because I wear glasses. I don't get good grades because I'm stupid. I don't deserve a promotion because I made a mistake on the last report.

It's a short, small step from finding the cause of problems and disappointments within ourselves to blaming ourselves for them. We somehow *deserve* to have these negative things happen to us—they come from failures within ourselves.

It is easy to see where we can go with this when we lose a child. My child has died. It must be my fault. Clearly, all the things that are wrong with me are the reason. I deserved this to happen.

I can *say* no—I did not deserve to have this happen. I can say it over and over. But still the small voice way deep inside of me says yes, I did, because. . . .

Fighting that voice takes a lot of energy—something most of us don't have an oversupply of when we face the death of our child. Yet I believe that this fight is essential.

None of us deserved to have this happen to us. No one deserves to lose a child.

AN UNFAMILIAR BODY

When you lose a child, your body all of a sudden becomes a stranger to you. This body that you know so well, that you dress and feed and care for, that you see in the mirror every morning as you brush your teeth, *looks* just like it always has. But looks are deceiving. Your body feels different. It acts differently. Your body is in shock.

One of the first things I noticed about myself when my son died was the terrible *physical* pain I experienced. It didn't stop. Mine was just below my rib cage, but yours can be anywhere: in your back, in your head, in your heart, in your stomach. The pain was with me most of my waking hours. It was so strong that I was doubled over at times, my fist pushing into the spot, as though counterpressure would ease it. I took pain medication. I sat, lay down, massaged it. Nothing helped. The pain was there, strong and hard.

I thought it would never go away. How can I live for years, I would wonder, with this much pain? Over time, slowly, it did go away. Sometimes, when I grieve very hard, it comes back for a while. But this happens less and less.

Now when I work with bereaved parents, I always ask them "Where is the pain, for you?" I see the relief in many faces, that someone else understands the pain. We expect the mental anguish. The physical pain surprises us, takes our breath away.

You may also notice immediately how often you are sighing. A deep intake of breath, held for a few moments, let out hopelessly. I sighed constantly in the early months of grieving. Still today, when I feel especially badly, I notice that my body, seemingly on its own, initiates the sighing process once again. Sighing is a common reaction to loss generally. For bereaved parents, this may become intense.

One of the general symptoms of shock that you may notice is a fluctuation in your normal body temperature. For weeks after the loss of my child, I shivered on and off uncontrollably. Sometimes, I shivered hard enough that my teeth rattled. I broke into cold sweats at times. It was hard to control the changes with clothing, or by turning up the thermostat. The cold was coming from inside me, and no external heat could alleviate it. Fortunately, as with the pain and the sighing, time will reduce both the frequency and the intensity.

Most bereaved parents' sleeping patterns are disrupted as well. Often we sleep a little, wake up and cry, sleep a little more. Many parents find that sleeping medication, prescribed by their physician, can help them to rest a little. Others find that they sleep much more than normal, as though the body is trying to protect the mind and emotions from the pain.

Our eating patterns also change. We cannot eat normally, and may gain or lose a great deal of weight. For some of us, eating eases sorrow on some primitive level. After all, food is love. We have lost a love, and need to fill the emptiness, and eat and eat. For others, the mere sight of food creates nausea. All that *life-sustaining* stuff reminds us that our child's life no longer needs sustenance. Elimination patterns are altered as well and diarrhea or constipation are common, adding to feelings of general malaise.

A physical reaction that I thought was unusual until I discussed it with other mothers and found it a common occurrence was "feeling" the loss in my womb. I had carried this child for nine months, and the loss was felt on a visceral level, almost independent of me. Even though my child was twenty-one years old when he died, I still experienced this reaction. When I realized what was happening, it made me sadder yet. For mothers who have lost a newborn, or had a miscarriage, this grieving, empty womb is often the focus of pain in a much more immediate way.

A CLOUDY MIND

When we lose a child, our minds are in shock as well as our bodies. Experienced parents look with sadness upon the newly bereaved, when they say that they are all right, that they accept what has happened and aren't suffering. They say they are eating and sleeping well, going to work, and engaging in all of their usual activities with little signs of strain. "They're shut down," the "older" parents say.

When we encounter more than our minds can take in, more than we can cope with, we "shut down" emotionally. This is our mind's defense against pain that is more than we can bear. When we're shut down, we don't seem able to feel anything. Some parents take this as a sign that they are coping well, while others worry about *why* they can't feel, why they don't cry and grieve.

If you believe that you are "shut down," you may find that you are fearful. What will happen, you wonder, when this period ends, and the full weight of the loss overwhelms you? What if you can't handle it? How long will it be before the shutdown wears off?

There are no quick answers to these questions. The only answer I know comes from my own experience: you will let in only what you can handle and no more. The shutdown doesn't end abruptly (thank goodness), but gradually, little by little. For some parents, the shutdown lasts weeks. For others, it may last months. A shutdown that does not seem to diminish may be a sign to you that there are other issues, besides the immediate one of your loss, which are causing the protective response to remain. If you are unable to feel the grief and pain after a year, it is best to seek professional help in addressing this problem. Unexpressed grief may manifest itself in many physical, mental, and emotional difficulties which may compound your problems.

One of the clearest and most common reactions to the loss of a child is a loss of memory—sometimes severe, sometimes mild. You forget simple things in the present: appointments, phone calls, minor responsibilities. Sometimes I would go to the grocery store and be unable to remember why I was there. Standing at the entrance in bewilderment, cart in hand, I tried to force my mind to recall what I needed. Not just once, but many times, I was unable to remember. And, of course, while I stood there, cart after cart of mothers and children walked past me, reminding me again and again of the reality of what I had lost.

Although my memory loss has improved over the years since the loss of my son, there are still lapses. I have learned to write everything down, often in duplicate. I take lists to the grocery store now; I used to shop from memory. I leave notes for myself ("Things I Must Do"); I used to remember without them.

It is also not uncommon to be unable to think through complicated arguments or situations. The mind of the bereaved parent, especially in the early months, is so focused on the loss of the child that there is little "room" for complex abstract thinking. This may cause difficulties at work. Be assured that this is not a permanent loss, and an understanding boss and staff can assist you greatly in dealing with this problem.

In certain situations it might be helpful to explain that you have recently lost a child, and that extra patience may be needed. I have never encountered anyone who has not been supportive and understanding when this explanation was given.

THE "WHY ME'S"

Is there ever a bereaved parent who does not ask: "Why me?" "Why my child?" "Why our family?" I don't think so. We want to believe that there is order, justice, and logic in the Universe. We want to believe there is a God, and that God is good. We want to believe that things always happen for a reason. But what reason can explain the loss of a child?

Often, you keep your questions hidden deep inside you. "Why me?," expressed, is too near to "Why not you?" And expressing "Why not you?" is unacceptable to most of us. And yet, deep in our heart of hearts, the "why me's" linger, painfully.

"He's a much worse father than I was, and his child is alive."

"She went to the same dance, was in the same car. Why is she all right and my child dead?"

"We were together all our pregnancies. I never smoke or drank and she even had a glass of wine sometimes. Why is her baby all right, when mine is dead?"

"All the kids played out in the street every day. Why did my child get run over? Look, they're *still* playing out there!"

"He was getting help for his problems. Why did he still kill himself?"

"There were so many people in the water. Why did the riptide take my child only?"

"There was no REASON. Why did they kill MY child?"

The question goes around and around in our heads. And, for most of us, there is no reason possible. Yet, giving up on reasons means giving up our entire way of thinking, and this is hard to do.

People around us also feel this urge to find reasons. Often they give us reasons:

"God wanted her to be one of his angels."

"The good always die young."

"He would have had terrible problems if he lived."

"It's nature's way of taking care of those who can't survive."

I am always tempted to answer, "Why didn't God want your child to be an angel?" "Is your child bad, then? Do you have to be bad to stay alive?" But most of the time I bite my tongue.

People don't mean to hurt us. They care, and want to help us. They don't know "why" either. Getting angry creates more anguish for us, offends them, and accomplishes little.

Sometimes the "why me's" overwhelm me, as I'm sure they overwhelm you. They get less frequent with time, but they're still there occasionally. Personally, I have decided there *is* no answer, at least none that I can know in this life. I believe it is not meant for me to know.

You will need to find some answer to this question that you can live with. The answer is yours alone, and comes from your own beliefs and thoughts and experiences.

THE NEED TO BLAME

Anger is a normal part of grieving. Along with thinking there must be a reason that our child has died, we also want to think there is someone or something we can hold accountable—someone to blame. Anger turned inward becomes guilt. Anger turned outward can become hatred.

If there is a clear person or cause involved in the death of our child, we can focus all of our anguish and hatred and fury on that person or thing:

"He was driving."

"She ran into her."

"He didn't watch carefully."

"She didn't follow the rules."

"They didn't stop him."

"He did it."

"They gave her the wrong medicine."

Having someone to blame gives us a focus, but it also gives us a pain that cannot be relieved. There is always the indisputable fact that he, she, or they are *alive* while your child is dead.

Not only are they alive, but often you may feel that they don't *care*. They are not suffering as you are. They are not being punished sufficiently for the death of your child.

Living with the anger that comes with having a clearly identifiable cause is often very destructive. I have worked with many parents whose anger has been so total that it has blocked out all grieving, and thus all movement, growth, or change. Although you may find this hard to believe, anger, while completely justifiable, can also be a way to ease the pain of your loss. If you're angry enough, there's no room to feel the sorrow.

Again and again, angry parents repeat the story of their child's accident, but the focus is not the loss of the child. It is on "that drunken bum," "that irresponsible teacher," "that driver, he was going 70 miles an hour," "that man should never have been paroled, he should have been left in jail forever," "that doctor didn't know what he was doing," "he didn't watch her like he was supposed to," "he just hit her and hit her."

There is no other feeling expressed or admitted. Surely, the loss of a child engenders many feelings, not just one! Remaining stuck in anger hurts *you* much more than the perpetrator. Although it is hard, and painful, it is important to try to let other emotions be felt: sadness, sorrow, grief—anger may be a part of emotions, but it cannot be the totality.

Juxtaposed to this, for some parents, is the Christian dictum which asks that we forgive. This may create religious issues that impact strongly on your mental state. If you find this to be a difficulty, you may need to seek pastoral help.

I have worked with parents who have been able to forgive. One couple's story remains in my mind for the supreme forgiveness they show. Their daughter was bludgeoned to death by her husband. The parents have both been able to forgive her murderer, and even to maintain a relationship with him as they raise their daughter's children. I stand in awe before the greatness of these parents: I know that I would be unable to do as they have done.

You must decide for yourself if you have a need to forgive. If you cannot, you need to be able to find a way to control or direct the force of your anger, for it will turn inward and destroy you.

One possible way to work with your anger is to try to seek justice, whether in terms of lawsuits, changes in policies, or other means. Ensuring that such deaths do not reoccur is one positive focus for your energy. You may lobby for a change in the laws, a road sign or traffic light, research on the medical cause of your child's death, or stringent standards for lifeguards, for example.

Another possible focus is working with others in circumstances similar to those of your child. Working with people with AIDS, the Multiple Sclerosis Society, or the Heart Association are possible examples.

Having an external person or persons to blame focuses your anger externally. You may have another, more painful direction for your anger: yourself, or your child.

Many parents blame themselves directly for the death of their child, and are overwhelmed with guilt. One parent with whom I have worked, for example, left her fourteen-month-old child unattended in the bathtub to answer the telephone, and returned to find that the baby had drowned. Another parent gave her child a bite of a hot dog. She was unable to dislodge it from the child's throat. Another parent allowed his teenage daughter to go to a party where he knew there would be drinking, and lost her when her drunken date drove in front of an oncoming train. Parents whose children commit suicide are especially vulnerable to self-blame, believing that they did not provide whatever their child needed to be happy. Parents who lose a child through miscarriage or stillbirth blame themselves, feeling that their bodies were unable to provide for the needs of the child growing within them.

Coming to terms with such direct responsibility is a difficult task. I think it is important to remember that you loved your child, and that accidents sometimes happen. Focusing on the good parenting that you provided may help you to deal with some of the self-blame. If you find yourself overwhelmed with guilt, you may need help.

Perhaps the most painful focus of blame can be your child.

"He knew he shouldn't run out in the street."

"How many times did I tell her not to take that shortcut back from school?"

"Why couldn't he get it together and stop being so depressed?"

"They knew they shouldn't speed!"

"He knew not to swim in the creek at night!"

"I told him and told him not to experiment with drugs!"

"I told her she should leave that guy!"

We have tried to protect our children from harm. We have watched over them, ferried them to activities, taught them safe bicycling and swimming, made sure they had good driving instruction, and encouraged good friends.

We gave them love and care and devotion. We gave them all that we could as parents. And still they didn't listen, didn't believe, didn't follow the rules we made. They were not careful; they took risks.

We blame them. But how can we? They died. They paid for the mistakes they made with their lives.

It is possible for me to blame my son. He broke his neck by diving in a too-shallow pool. He *knew* it was too shallow. I had told him and told him, over the years, hundreds of times, not to jump in shallow pools. He did it anyway.

Another parent's son died when an unshored trench he was working in collapsed on him. Over and over, this parent had warned her child never to work in an unshored trench, that there was the danger of collapse. Yet, when asked to go, he went in, and the trench collapsed.

Another parent struggled with her child's sexual activities, accepting the behavior, but begging her to be careful, to use protection. Her daughter did not think she needed protection, and contracted the AIDS virus.

We warn our children never to drink and drive. We tell them we will come to get them, anytime, anywhere, no questions asked. And yet, how often do teenagers lose their lives when they or their friends drive under the influence of alcohol?

And how often do we tell our children never, never to speak to strangers? But strangers can be beguiling, and a child may forget the warning.

I have found that it is not helpful to blame my child. Like so many young people, he believed it could never happen to him. The young think that they are invincible, indestructible, eternal, and that nothing can ever happen to them. Death is far, far away when we are young. I think it is meant to be that way, for risk and adventure are an important part of what these years offer each young person. Chances are many other young people of all ages may have done what your child has done and have come to no harm. Yours did. Mine did. I can't hold him responsible for that any more than those parents whose children came to no harm hold them responsible for the same acts.

If your child has chosen to end his or her own life, these arguments do not work well, for in these cases, whether they wanted to succeed or were only crying for help, there was some intention on the child's part to end his or her life. Both blame and guilt are often very strong, and often overwhelming for parents. Children who choose to end their lives are in terrible pain, either mental or physical. Mental pain, I believe, can be as strong, if not stronger, than physical pain. If your child, with the more limited wisdom of fewer years, could see no way out of the pain in this life, can you truly blame her or him for seeking to end it in the only way he or she knew? Suicide is perhaps one of the most difficult deaths for those left behind, especially parents. I discuss these issues further in Chapter 8.

We are overwhelmed. We are trying to understand what has happened, but we see it in the context of our own personal experiences, our parenting histories, our self-doubts and fears and worries, our anger, and our blame and guilt. Too much floods into our beings, and we feel a loss of control which terrifies us. We may feel that we are unable to control ourselves, or function "normally" in any aspect of our daily lives.

All of these problems with our minds and bodies and feelings sometimes make us think that we are crazy. Bereaved parents often express that belief or fear. For the overwhelming majority of us, this is not true. We are experiencing "normal" reactions to a severe shock, a pain beyond imagining. But we are not mentally ill!

CHAPTER THREE

MARRIAGE:
THE SOBERING FACTS

Sometime in the first few days after the death of my son, several friends, none of whom, of course, I remember, took me aside and told me a very sobering fact:

> The divorce rate
> for bereaved parents
> is over 80%
> during the first five years after the loss of a child.

This meant nothing to me in those first few weeks. I was in shock, overwhelmed, in pain. I could hardly move. I knew there were people around me but I didn't really relate to anyone.

When we had our first fights over our son and his death, the information I had stored somewhere in the recesses of my brain leapt out at me: over 80%.

That's a very high number.

BEATING THE ODDS IS A BIG JOB

I remember making a conscious choice to try to beat the odds. The very first thing I did was to sit down with my husband and share this statistic. Two of us had to work on this if we were going to make it. We had to make a commitment to work with each other and to try to maintain communication no matter how hard it became.

If you can make it to the five-year mark, the odds decrease dramatically. You will still need to be careful, but the solid work you have done in those first years will serve as a good foundation for you.

WHAT YOU BRING WITH YOU

• Your Marital Relationship

If you are married at the time of your loss, you bring with you a marital history as well as a personal one. This history is very complex and involves many different aspects of your relationship. The length of time you have been married, and whether this is your first, second, or third marriage, are only the easiest, not necessarily the most important, things to consider.

Every marriage is different: each couple has a unique style that evolves during the marriage. Each comes to the marriage with personal experiences and events, relationships, and, during the course of the marriage, continues to grow and change as an individual. But beyond the two separate entities is something that transcends them, something that has an identity of its own. There is the husband, there is the wife, and there is the marriage.

You may find it helpful to think about this third entity, the marriage, and explore some of its characteristics. Look at the strengths and weaknesses, the quality of the interaction, what seems to "work" within the marriage, and what doesn't. The better you understand your marital relationship, the better your chance of "beating the odds."

To help you look at these issues, a few areas that are important in assessing your relationship might be considered.

A good place to begin to explore is your style of communication with each other about important subjects. Do you each communicate in very different ways, and often feel frustrated, shut out, overwhelmed? Do each of you feel free to bring up issues that are troubling you? Do you have open discussions that involve specific ideas and decisions? Or does much of your communicating get done without words—with silences, gestures, body language? Do you "read" each other's nonverbal communication well? Can you share feelings with one another—not just joy and happiness and love but also pain, humiliation, frustration, anger, disappointment? Do you each support the other, or does one partner feel unsupported, ignored, unheard?

What are the themes of your marriage? What are your mutual goals? What are the best moments, and what are the worst? What do each of you find difficult in the relationship? What kinds of things upset each of you about the other?

Looking at the way you share decision-making in your marriage can also be helpful. Who makes the decisions when you disagree? Do you each make decisions in different areas? For example, who decides how money will be spent? Where to go on vacation? What to do Saturday night? Where you live? What jobs you take? When and how to have sex? When to see the relatives? Whether you will pursue separate personal interests, and when? What religious organization you will belong to, and how often you will attend? Does one person make the major decisions, the other the minor ones? When there are disagreements, who generally gives in?

Do each of you have clearly defined roles? Do you help each other as needed, even if the job is not your role, such as housecleaning, lawn mowing, breadwinning, child care? Is one of you always the martyr? The clown? The person with all the answers?

Is there cultural, ethnic, religious conguity between you, or are there differences? How do these impact on your relationship? Whose culture, traditions, church, language becomes the dominant one in the relationship?

Thinking through some of these issues in your marriage is not something you'll be able to do at one sitting. Sometimes, it's not so much a question of making a list and checking off who does what, when, and how, as it is of opening your eyes and ears and mind and heart and just becoming *aware* of the way that your marriage functions.

Once you think that you have some grasp of how your marriage works, look long and hard at its strengths and weaknesses. How can you use the strengths to beat the odds? How can you minimize the weaknesses?

Many couples encounter the death of a child from within an already troubled marriage. The loss of the child may serve as a catalyst for these couples: deciding to separate or to work to stay together becomes more urgent when the stresses and strains of bereavement pull at your relationship.

Other couples may find that there are special feelings that may come from the kind of "official" relationship the parent had with the child. Biological parent, foster parent, adoptive parent, and stepparent may relate to the loss differently. This can place an additional strain on the marriage during an already difficult time.

While I have used the term "marriage" throughout this book, these concepts can apply equally to any other relationship of two adults who, together, were involved in the care of the child who has died.

• Your Parenting Roles

When you have children, your marriage exists, at least in part, within the context of a family relationship, so that parenting roles become an important part of your relationship.

Few, if any, parents agree, always and completely, on how to raise a child. There are bound to be differences. Each parent enters the parenting role with different role models (his or her own parents), different experiences in being parented, different life experiences, and often different styles of communicating and relating to others. We don't parent exactly the same way, and this inescapable fact has a strong effect on our relationship.

We tend not to spend equal time parenting. One parent usually has the primary responsibility for child care. Although many families have two parents who work outside the home, who is it that leaves work when a child is ill? Who drives the children to after-school activities? Who helps with homework? Who is the primary disciplinarian?

Problems arise when there are conflicts between the parents regarding how the children are to be raised. Curfews, use of cars, homework, friends, bedtime, personal hygiene, chores, dating, and literally thousands of other issues require that rules be made, followed, and enforced. One parent may be more liberal than the other. One may be more lax about enforcement. Children notoriously prefer to follow the rules of the liberal, lax parent, and this creates conflict in the family between parents and between parents and children.

Our personalities and the personalities of our children interact with a chemistry that is distinct but variable. One child relates more intensely to one parent because of a similarity in personality, interests, and temperament, while another may feel closer to the other parent. We also relate to each of our children differently: each child may experience us as parents differently due not only to personal character traits, but also to the child's gender, age, and position in the family. We may *love* all of our children equally, but we don't relate to them all in the same way.

Out of these interwoven, sometimes open and sometimes covert systems within each of our families, roles and relationship patterns emerge. One parent may be the comforter in times of distress, another may be the adviser about schools and careers. One may be the family organizer, the other the one who brings a touch of humor to tense situations. One may deal well in crises, another can stand by for the long haul. Children quickly learn the role of each parent, and so develop a different relationship with each.

When a child dies, parents experience the loss differently. Each will experience it within the context of his or her own unique relationship to that child. This is foundational in understanding the different ways in which parents grieve.

Because parents have different ideas about child-rearing, there will have been, over the period of the life of the child, disagreements between them regarding the rearing of that child. The death of the child exacerbates, rather than resolves, such disagreements. Accusations fly:

"You didn't discipline her enough."

"You let him run wild."

"You were always so critical of him."

"You punished him too hard."

"You kept her all to yourself."

"You never did anything with him, spent time with him."

"You got him that bike when I told you he was too young."

"You always babied her."

All parents have these kinds of arguments. The difference, I think, is that there is time for parents who have not lost their child to resolve them, time to see, usually, that their child turned out all right after all in spite of whatever the other parent might have done "wrong."

We do not have that chance. Our arguments stay frozen in time. Year after year, we repeat them endlessly, hopelessly. They are unresolvable.

All we can do, all we MUST do, in the interest of beating those odds, is to lay them aside, give up, let go.

Each of us has parented with love. Each of us has parented in the way that we thought was best for our child. Each of us made the best decisions possible with the knowledge and experience that we had at the time. We could have done no more. Forgive yourself. Forgive each other.

GRIEVING TOGETHER, GRIEVING APART

In the first weeks after I lost my child, I was not aware of anyone's grief but my own. Grief overwhelmed me, filled up every nook and cranny of my soul, and blocked out everything and everyone else. I don't know what my husband did. I was not aware.

I know that he stood beside me at the funeral, and held my hand most of the time we were in public. I know I rested my head on his shoulder at times, and that he put his arms around me.

It seemed as though we were parallel grieving, in the same way that toddlers parallel play. It was comforting that he was there, in a way. We didn't want to be apart, but we didn't share much of our feelings.

I discovered that I needed to talk. Like many bereaved parents, I needed to tell the story over and over and over again. I needed to cry each time and to be comforted each time. I felt as though I was a bottomless well of tears and stories that never ended. I told the story several times a day in the early months.

This required a constant supply of willing listeners. My husband was not one of them. First of all, he already *knew* the story. There wasn't much I could tell him that he hadn't experienced directly. Second, I needed someone who would say the comforting words as I spoke. He could not comfort me. He was grieving too hard himself, in his own way. Third, I believe it hurt him more to listen to my pain—it made his own worse. It fueled his frustration and his anger.

Role-cast as most men are by society's expectations, my husband had a difficult time with tears and emotions. His grief was very private, and he could not share. He did not want, or seem to need, to repeat the story. He closed himself up within himself; he erected internal barriers to the pain.

I believe our story is not untypical of many parents who have lost a child. Women have a tendency to express feelings and emotions. They turn readily to other women for help and support. Men see the expression of sorrow, grief, and often even joy and happiness as a weakness, and tend to avoid such expression, especially in the presence of others.

For many parents, grieving apart becomes a pattern that is rarely broken. Some cry alone in the car, some on their beds, some behind closed office doors. Some cry without tears. Some hold a tight knot of pain within themselves, while others seem to dissolve into hysteria frequently.

Just as we have different character traits, and different life experiences from our mates, so too do we grieve differently.

It is a lesson that is often painful to learn. When we are hurt, it seems natural to turn to the person closest to us. We expect understanding and support, no matter which way our grief expresses itself. But different ways of grieving often make it difficult for spouses to receive this help from each other.

It begins very slowly, but after weeks or months you may notice that your grief seems manageable, even slightly lessened, for a few minutes, then maybe for an hour, an afternoon, a day. During most of the first year, you have "up" days, and "down" days. Your "up" days are very fragile, and the slightest problem will send you back into seemingly bottomless grief. Invariably, parents say that they are having a "down" day when their spouse is having an "up" day, and vice versa.

Because the "up's" are often hard to achieve and harder to sustain, we are very vulnerable during these times. A "down" spouse can quickly destroy that momentary inner peace. It is almost impossible to help a "down" spouse get "up," while it is very easy to plummet an "up" spouse back into painful grief.

Because people manifest grief differently, it is not uncommon for one spouse to feel that he or she is suffering more, is in more pain, and misses the child more than the other. Anger and resentment against that seemingly less-suffering spouse seems to come from nowhere, and hurting words are often spoken. Sometimes no words are spoken, and the resentment-laden silence deepens with each passing day.

Of course you will grieve differently than your spouse. That doesn't mean your spouse does not grieve as deeply, however. Both spoken words and silences denote a terrible pain.

Your spouse may not be able to help you grieve, but he needs dearly to know that you recognize that he is in pain. That joint, mutual recognition of your tragedy, and the protectiveness that comes with it, is the bridge upon which your relationship must build.

BUILDING BRIDGES ON OLD FOUNDATIONS

It may feel sometimes that your marriage is stretched to its very limits. You can feel the strain placed upon it by your loss every day, and this fresh sorrow overlays an already over-burdened heart.

How do you reach out? How do you build a bridge across the silence, across the tears that spring fresh with every thought of your child? How do you find any meaning, any joy, any hope in your future together?

The bricks that you need to rebuild are all around you. Though the bridge is broken, all of the pieces are there, waiting for your hands to pick them up, return them to their place, and hold them together with a new mortar, one that contains within it the knowledge of the loss of your child.

If you try to build the bridge without your partner's help, it will never reach the other side. If you try to build it as it was, without the knowledge of your mutual loss, the bricks will not hold together. If you try to build it only out of need, without love and compassion, the bricks will crumble in your hands.

Only your hands together can rebuild. Only you can find within yourselves the desire, and the will, to keep and treasure and preserve this relationship. Your marriage was just the two of you, above and beyond *any* other relationship. It still is. Only you can keep it that way.

ALONE AGAIN, ANOTHER LOSS

Sometimes, though we try and try, we cannot hold our marriage intact. Sometimes, by our own choice or by that of our mate, we find ourselves facing a new loss and a new, different kind of pain. The two pains dance with each other, intertwine, and twirl apart, tearing us to pieces with every move.

Whether you are the one who leaves, or the one who is left behind, the pain is overwhelming. Parenthood and marriage are our two most important, basic roles. Failing at one is a tragedy. Losing at both seems to destroy, at least for a time, our entire selves.

We often define ourselves by our roles: husband, father, wife, mother. These come before careers, interests, and abilities. These are the roles that define us as human beings, that define our relationship to the human family. To lose them may leave us without an identity, without a reason for being.

The bricks are there, but there is no bridge possible. The only way forward is to use the bricks to build a new structure, one that defines this person that you now are, with strengths and weaknesses, pains and sorrows, and with something else that all builders after the loss of a child must have—the knowledge of the possibility of joy at some future time and place.

Losing a child and a marriage is more than most parents can face without professional help. If you find yourself unable to cope, overwhelmed and immobilized, depressed and angry, there are many community services available to help you to deal both with your feelings and with the practical matters that you may find confusing and unfamiliar.

CHAPTER FOUR

OUR OTHER CHILDREN

THE "FORGOTTEN MOURNERS"

The death of a brother or a sister has an enormous impact on siblings of any age. Often, in the first throes of pain and despair, parents are unable to cope with trying to understand and help their other children to understand what has happened.

Family and friends tend to focus on the grief of the parents, generally, rather than that of the other children in the family. I think this may be due to several factors, not the least of which are that adults can communicate more easily with other adults, can empathize with adults more easily, and are unsure of what the parents have told the children or what they would want them to be told.

Some parents believe that it is best for the other children to be shielded from exposure to the death of a brother or sister. However, research has shown that children will make a much healthier adjustment to the loss of a brother or sister if they are informed and allowed to participate, as their age permits, in the events. Children who are sent away to family or neighbors around the time of death may experience stronger feelings of abandonment, exclusion, and separation anxiety. Rather, they need to feel that they are safe and secure within the family.

BEREAVED SIBLINGS

Your other children have suffered a loss perhaps as severe as your own. It differs in quality, perhaps, as their relationship with the dead child differed from yours. However, they, like you, are experiencing both the loss and the change that the loss brings to the structure and functioning of your family.

Much of a family's energy, as a whole, is focused around the children and the child-rearing process. Your entire family system has suffered a shock with the loss of your child. The patterns of relationships between parents, parents and children, and children with each other are all severely affected. How your family integrates this loss into the family system will depend on several factors, such as previous history of dealing with loss, the nature and circumstances of the child's death (long illness, hospice care, accident, suicide, etc.), the position and function of the child in the family system ("the baby," "the clown," "the one who gets in trouble," etc.), your family's religious and spiritual beliefs, and patterns of communication within your family.

The child in the family nearest in age to the dead child is often the most at risk for behavior, school, physical, and other problems. Such a child may over-identify with the dead child, and try to live that child's life, as well as her own. She may feel the presence of the dead child around her, have dreams, fantasies, or report somatic experiences of the dead child's presence. She may also idealize the dead child, and her relationship with him.

Children who have shared a room with a dead child have a special set of problems, and parents often agonize over what to do with a dead child's belongings, a task that is especially hard when these are in the room with another child. The solution to these difficulties depends upon the very unique qualities of your own family and the relationship of the roommates. Some parents feel that they must immediately remove all traces of the dead child from the room of her sibling. Some let things remain as the dead child left them, and prefer that the sibling, now alone in the room, not touch or disturb anything. It is best to discuss this issue with your child, and be guided by what appears comfortable to her. Removing her from the decision-making process about something as personal as her room may create resentment, anger, and an increased feeling of helplessness for a child already struggling to deal with these difficult emotions.

Your bereaved child may want to wear the dead child's clothing for a while, use her toys, books, sporting equipment, car, or sit at her place at dinner. This most often occurs in the first months, the "transition months" when your family is still working hard to accept and reconcile the loss into the family's experience. These concrete evidences of a child's existence may help your son or daughter to understand and deal with the loss. If your child continues to be extremely tied to the dead child's belongings after a year, you may want to initiate counseling. Such an extreme reaction may be a sign of deeper difficulties for your child in dealing with his loss.

The loss of a child may impact strongly on your relationships with your other children. One common problem is that the extent and depth of your grief is interpreted as a lack of love for him/them. "After all," the child reasons, "I'm here. Dad doesn't seem to care. He is quiet and withdrawn and won't even talk to me. Mom cries all the time. Isn't she happy she still has ME? I always thought she loved him more, and now I really know it. She just doesn't care about me!" It is hard for us to imagine that a surviving child may be jealous of a dead sibling, but this is a common occurrence.

I know that I did spend more of my time grieving than I spent on my other two children during the first months. It took some time before I could say to myself that my dead child occupied roughly one third of my time and attention while alive, and that it was important that I try to give him only one third of my time and attention now that he was dead. I needed to let my other children in. I believe that it is difficult to do this at first, but with time and effort I know that it is possible. And I know that it is worth the effort, for our surviving children need us and have much to give.

Almost every parent observes serious and often severe reactions on the part of their living children to the death of a sibling. One common reaction is guilt: guilt for being alive; guilt for not having done, cared, sacrificed enough; guilt for not having suffered; guilt from old arguments; and guilt from hidden secret wishes that the now-dead sibling would, in fact, go away, and leave the room, TV, parent, car, and so forth to the remaining child. Although common, such guilt is often a complex of deep and painful feelings, which the child may have difficulty understanding or accepting.

Another very common reaction of surviving siblings is anger. Anger may be focused on the dead child, the parent, God, the cause of death (driver of the car, illness and/or doctor, boss, for example). However, anger may also be unfocused—not tied to any specific person, thing, or event. This "free-floating" anger may be expressed both in words and actions. Physically, a teenage boy may bash holes in the wall, break down a door, or tear a favorite shirt in a effort to express his anger. Verbally, a child may yell and scream about a friend, a teacher, an event at school, the anger seeming a great over-reaction to the actual event. Sometimes, anger may be focused toward you.

Your surviving children may feel that you are somehow to blame for the death of your child. They may accuse you, verbally or nonverbally, of the same things of which you accuse yourself, plus a few of their own. They may feel that you were too strict, overcritical, or too forgiving; that you encouraged risk-taking, overprotected, yelled too much, ignored symptoms or complaints of illness, made the dead child (and often themselves too) feel guilty or inferior or stupid, favored or didn't favor, and so forth. Their criticisms, if verbal, sting, and, worse than that, reinforce our own self-criticism and self-blame.

We want our surviving children to reassure us that we have been good parents, that we are not to blame for what has happened. We want them to help us to push away our own doubts about our parenting. Instead, they reinforce them.

Our children's accusations may not be verbalized for a long time—weeks, months, or years. We may think that our families are pulling together, when, in fact, they are tearing apart in unseen and unlikely places.

Recognizing that this reaction on the part of your surviving children is not unusual may help you. They, too, need to find someone, or something, to blame. We are handy targets, especially since we are 1) like all parents, not perfect, 2) viewed as powerful, and 3) very involved with all of our children.

It is important to help your children express all of their feelings of anger and resentment, even if these are directed at you. If you feel that you are unable to handle listening to their accusations, when you yourself are grieving and blaming yourself, you may want to suggest that counseling might be helpful to them. With time, most surviving children understand that you did not directly and willfully cause your child's death.

Bereaved siblings are also often easily frustrated and impatient, quick to blame and accuse, and aggressive with peers and classmates. Mood swings may leave your children furious one minute and in tears the next.

Your children may also seek comfort temporarily in an intact family. Your child may turn to the families of aunts, uncles, and cousins; families of their friends and schoolmates; the family of a member of your church or synagogue; or the family next door. These families have the warmth, joy, and wholeness that you have lost. There is an unbroken tie between family members. Your child misses the good times, the family activities and banter, the sense of wholeness that your family has lost. He knows that the other family cannot replace his own, cannot heal his, or your, broken heart. But, for the time that he is with them, at least, he may be able to set the grieving aside and temporarily resume the exuberance and joys of his own childhood experience, from which he has been so tragically severed by his sibling's death.

If our child had more than one sibling, we may want to think that our surviving siblings will support each other, love each other, have understanding and compassion for each other. And they generally do. But not all the time.

Our children have, over the course of their lives, established certain ways of relating to each other. These patterns included the sibling who died. The loss is not only a personal one for each child. It is also a loss of familiar, well-accepted, comfortable relationship patterns. Each child must find a new place in the constellation that has, so sadly, lost a shining star.

When my son died, my younger daughter became the baby. She had spent her entire life since his birth complaining about being the middle child. She hated it, she said. It was like not having any identity. First got to do everything earlier; last got special attention for being the youngest. The middle was a nothing place.

Yet she grieved hard and painfully, not only for her brother, but for her lost place in the family. She realized that there was a security in being in the middle. She didn't want to be the youngest child. That was not part of her definition of who she was.

You may also find that your children's relationship to each other changes with the loss of their sibling. Your children had reached some sort of equilibrium among themselves, and this equilibrium is gone. The old rules don't hold anymore, and there are no new ones at first.

And, there's all the anger and pain and frustration of the loss which they, too, are feeling. With little awareness of the emotions and changes going on inside them, you may find that your children argue and fight much more than they used to, ignore each other when they used to share, or withdraw from any meaningful conversations. This may continue for months or years. After all, it took their whole lives to develop the relationships they had had. You cannot expect that they will readjust them so quickly.

All this is very painful for you, the parent. You've had a terrible loss. You desperately want your surviving children to be close, to share and love and comfort each other. Instead, you find them arguing, ignoring, complaining. You may find that you become the mediator, the listener, though every angry word that you hear opens new wounds in an already bleeding heart.

Try to encourage your children to communicate directly, without you. You need to get out of the middle and let them work out new patterns. As you were not a part of them before, so you cannot be a part of them now. With time, your children will find new ways to relate.

Unless the bereaved siblings are themselves adults with good self-awareness, they may be unaware of the source of their guilt, anger, frustration, or other emotion. They may be confused, and fearful of their own reactions, especially of their own violence. This may cause them to withdraw in an attempt to control their behavior, to try to "put a lid on it," so that neither they themselves nor you will be aware of their inner turbulence.

You may notice a drop in school performance, a separation from old friends, an unwillingness to meet new people, or other signs that she is struggling with this devastating tragedy.

Your other children may be willing to discuss some of these feelings and reactions and behaviors with you, or they may not. It it vital to their mental health, and to their relationship with you, that you remain open and accepting of the emotions that are buffeting them, if not always accepting of the behaviors. An open line of communication with you, a sense of support, reassurance that their behavior is understandable, and some limits placed on extreme behavior if necessary will best help your child to deal with his loss.

In this chapter, I've tried to address some of the special needs of siblings who are bereaved at different ages. However, it is important for you as a parent to understand that your child will pass through many stages as she grows and matures, and that issues and answers that seemed appropriate for one age do not address the needs and problems of another. You may help your three-year old to understand and accept the loss of his baby brother, but find that he needs different support and explanations at ten, or at fourteen, or at thirty. Life cycle changes and events also often cause old unresolved or poorly understood issues to surface. Marriage, birth of a child, death of a friend or parent—all of these can renew old anxieties, angers, and grief. You need to be aware that your child's need to work through issues surrounding the loss of his sibling will continue, and recur, at many times during his life.

Many, if not most, bereaved siblings may need professional help with these problems, sometimes for an extended period of time. They may ask you for help, or you may offer it, as you discuss the difficulties your child is experiencing. Problems may surface immediately, but it is not unusual for bereaved siblings to show greater signs of distress after a (supposedly) "good" initial adjustment. It may be three, four, five, or more years before your other children become able to express some of their guilt and anger over their loss.

THE YOUNG CHILD

Children's reactions to the loss of a brother or sister differ from yours. Their ability to understand death is different, as is their ability to express their feelings about the loss. Young children easily misunderstand what has happened and why. If these misunderstandings continue, they may have serious problems later in life.

At a time when you yourself can barely manage to function, you may find it especially difficult to help your young child. He may show no outward reaction, and continue to play, eat, and sleep as usual. Overwhelmed with your own emotions, you may feel relieved that the child appears to be adjusting so well, and pay little attention to the more subtle signs of distress. Avoidance, or denial, of what has happened is as unhealthy for the child as it is for you. You may need to explain gently to the child what has happened, even without being asked, and encourage the child to ask questions and share his or her feelings. It is helpful to hold the child on your lap, or sit nearby, touching the child to communicate a sense of safety and security.

If your child does not seem interested in talking about what has happened, it is best not to force her to listen repeatedly. Just let her know that you are there, whenever the child is ready.

On the other hand, he may be preoccupied with the death—and ask over and over and over again for you to tell the "story" of what has happened. Don't be impatient—your child is looking for consistency and reassurance, and security in the knowledge that the rest of the family is safe and will remain together. Keep the story clear and very simple, use words that your child understands, and answer questions truthfully. Your child needs to be able to trust you, and the simple truth is the best way to encourage this.

Death is a new concept for most young children. The permanence of death is often not understood, and the child may continue to ask when the dead child will return. Although this may be painful to you, it is important to explain in a way that the child will understand that the dead child will not be returning home.

One of the hardest questions to answer is "but where *is* she?" You can answer this simply from your own beliefs.

"Jane is in heaven."

"George is with Jesus."

"Stewie is with the angels, helping them."

"Jessie is in the ground helping the flowers to grow."

"Allie is with the Great Spirit."

Answering from within your own beliefs allows you to provide more explanations, if needed, comfortably. In the section entitled "But Where Is My Sister? What Happened?" below, I have suggested some answers that are NOT helpful to children of any age, and the reasons they are not.

If it is true for you, you may need to say "I don't know" and to help your child to understand that there are some things that we can't know in this world.

Young children will accept a very simple explanation much more easily that a complex, thorough, detailed story. You will need to repeat it again and again, as long as the child needs to hear it.

THE SCHOOL-AGED CHILD

School-aged children are at a more advanced developmental stage and may be more persistent in asking for detailed information. They may question what is told to them. They are also hearing explanations from other children at school and will need reassurance from you to deal with these.

Because school-aged children have a clearer understanding of permanence and death, they may have more anxiety, depression, fear, and physical symptoms than younger children. There is an awareness of mortality, and the knowledge that, if it happened to Joey, it could happen to me as well. If Joey died after an illness, a school-aged child may become overly concerned about "catching" a disease. Even a cold may appear very threatening, as possibly the carrier of her own death.

School-aged children are also able to reason about more complex issues and may have a great deal of guilt over the death of a sibling. The child's understanding of causation, usually inaccurate, can cause agony for a school-aged sibling.

"I had a fight with her, and then she died."

"I wouldn't let him use my bat, and then he died."

"I wanted to have a room of my own and now he is dead."

"I hit her so hard, she died."

"I wanted Mommy to stay with me and not go to the hospital and he died."

"I wanted her to go away and never come back because she was always taking my toys and messing things up and now she did go away."

Guilt such as this may be crippling to a child, and leave traces which can be carried into adulthood. It is important to help your child to express his belief about what happened, and to gently reassure him that he did not cause the sibling's death.

THE ADOLESCENT

Teenagers' developmental tasks are different than those of younger children, and often create special problems when a sibling dies. Teenagers are often overwhelmed with their own struggles in growing and maturation, and have a difficult time integrating this loss into them. They are working hard at independence and separation, at mastering their bodies and understanding their thoughts. It is difficult to reconcile this striving toward independence with grieving. They are learning roles, and mourning is often a completely unfamiliar one to them. They do not know how to act, and because of this it may seem to us that they are unaffected by the loss of their sibling.

Teens need opportunities to talk, explanations, reassurance, and support, but they also need privacy and time alone. This is a time when adults are often mistrusted, and teens may prefer to turn to their peers for help when a brother or sister dies. Often, parents feel cut off from the emotional experiences of their teen in dealing with the death.

Too often, I hear parents of teens saying,

"I hope he's talking to somebody. He sure isn't talking to me."

"She acts like nothing happened. All she cares about is her clothes and her dates and her friends."

You cannot force a teen to turn to you for help. You can be available, reassuring, and understanding.

Like you, teens can deny what has happened, and pretend that everything is just as it used to be. They also may feel guilt or responsibility, as school-aged children do. One young man was out with a brother and several friends. They were involved in a severe automobile accident. His brother was thrown from the car and was unconscious when he rushed to him. Frantic, he tried CPR, recently learned during a school health course. He was unable to revive his brother and blames himself as the cause of his death.

Studies have shown that teens experience the loss of a brother or sister most severely 6 to 12 months after the death, and again at 18 to 24 months, with girls having more anxiety and health issues than boys. Teens may have difficulties at school, with social relationships, at work, with their health, or with family relationships.

Because of their developmental stage, counseling may be necessary following the loss of a sibling, often of several years' duration. When the death is a result of suicide, more extensive help is often needed. The teen years are high-risk years for suicide, and the loss of a brother or sister in this way may reinforce and encourage a teen's own feelings in this direction.

THE ADULT CHILD

Your adult child may be living out of the home, may be married, and may have children of his own. The child's own social constellation, his place in your family, his relationship with you, and his relationship with the dead child all impact greatly on his grieving. Like you and your younger children, the adult child needs support, reassurance, and a sense of safety. He also needs a time and place to mourn.

An adult child who has a limited social constellation and minimal support may find that the loss of a sibling impacts very strongly. There is ample time for grieving, for anger, for a sense of loneliness and abandonment. On the other hand, the adult child with multiple family and job responsibilities may find that there is little time to sort through his emotions, and that others have little understanding for what he is experiencing. Understanding, support, and adequate time to grieve are important to adult children.

Family patterns and relationships, which may fluctuate while children are in the home, are generally fixed when a child leaves home. Patterns have been reinforced by many years of experience. Was big sister another parent to the dead child? Did younger brother always follow big brother, turn to him for advice? Did he resent the younger child's place in the family? Did big brother protect little sister? Did he join with other siblings to tease?

Just as your parenting patterns strongly affect how you interpret and respond to the loss of your child, and your relationship with your mate, brothering and sistering patterns impact greatly on your children. Just as your arguments, disagreements, and problems remain fixed in time when your child dies, incapable of being resolved, so do those of your adult child. There may be regrets about arguments or rivalries. These cannot be resolved directly.

If you had three or more children, the loss of a child can affect the remaining children's relationship with each other. Was one child closer to the dead child than another? Did one feel left out? Picked on? Ignored? Helping adult children to change unhealthy relationship patterns with each other is vitally important to their own mental health and well-being.

As a bereaved parent, you agonize over these problems. You have lost a child. You *need* your surviving child(ren) to be healthy, happy, and loving. You need them to get along, so that you can try to maintain some family relationships. You are more aware than before of how important family relationships are and you feel fragile and vulnerable.

Perhaps even more painful is the disruption that the death of a child can cause in your relationship with your other child(ren). Old accusations of favoritism, old disapprovals, old resentments, old arguments come back strong and fresh. Your child is trying to deal with a maelstrom of emotions, and often needs a focus of anger and blame. You may become that focus, at least temporarily. At a time when you are most vulnerable and most in need of support, your adult child may not only deny you that support, but actively seem to want to cause further disruption and pain in the family. Maintaining good communication may be helpful in dealing with this issue with your adult child.

Adult children who are themselves parents may be able to empathize with you much more strongly. They know how terrible your loss is. They may give you a great deal of support, but they may have serious problems of their own as well.

Just as your faith in goodness and justice and God may be shaken, so may your child's. He *knows* that death can come—instantly and silently, slowly and painfully—he knows it is possible. If he identifies with you, he may transfer your loss onto a fear of a similar one. He may worry over his children constantly. He may feel that Fate has terrible grief in store for him.

You may find that your adult child develops ways of coping with the loss that are troublesome. She may drink more heavily, take undue risks, withdraw from friends and social activities, sleep long hours or too little, become aggressive or overly argumentative, or develop other behavior problems.

Adult children, too, may need professional help to work through some of the family issues that are affecting their self-perception, their relationship with other family members, and their ability to understand and accept their loss.

"BUT WHERE IS MY SISTER? WHAT HAPPENED?"

Each family and child is different, and you know best how to answer your child's questions. Asking questions is a very healthy reaction on the part of your child—it shows that she understands that something has happened, and needs your help to clarify why and how. It is always best to be gentle, truthful, and reassuring.

Your answers need to be clear and appropriate to the age of the child who is asking. Too much information, or too little, can create anxiety in bereaved siblings at all ages. The four-year-old child may need a simple sentence, repeated frequently, while the adult about to get married may want complex medical explanations that also involve heredity, genetic predisposition, mental status, behavior and personality issues, and others. Each is asking out of his own growth needs, and should be answered appropriately but always honestly, truthfully, and with love and support.

Some answers should *not* be used, as they increase rather than alleviate anxiety in your child.

"Mary went to sleep," for example, can create night-time problems for many children. A child can easily become frightened of falling asleep, afraid that he, too, will die like Mary did. "If it can happen to Mary, it can happen to me," the child will reason, quite logically, "so I better stay awake and never go to sleep!" It is easy to see the sleep disorders that can follow upon such an explanation. Additionally, the child knows that he wakes up from sleep. Mary, too, he reasons, will wake up and come back. Equating something transient like sleep with something permanent like death, while seeming to offer a peaceful answer, actually confuses and upsets your child.

Another answer to avoid is "Tommy was so good, God took him to be an angel." A whole variety of problems can be created in the child's mind with this answer. She might wonder if, since God took Tommy and not her, God does not think that she is good, and begin to believe that she must be bad. Or, she might worry that if she is good, God will come and take her away too. She might even wonder if she should *want* to be taken away to be an angel, since that is assumed to be a good thing to have happen. You can see these and other problems easily creating anxiety, fears, and stress in children.

A variation on this theme also to be avoided is "God loved Janey and took her." Again, imagine what a child can do with this idea. If God loves you, the child can wonder, does he come and take you away? If God took Janey and not me, does that mean that God does not love me? Why does God love Janey and not me? If I want to stay here at home with my family, should I want God *not* to love me?

While these explanations may be comforting to parents, they create anxieties in children. As adults, we have a different understanding of God, the hereafter, and death than young children do. Even if your family attends church, synagogue, or temple regularly, and God is a comfortable daily part of your child's life, the associations your child can make with these kinds of explanations can cause psychological harm.

It is important not only that you avoid these kinds of explanations yourself but that you try as best you can to shield your child from the facile and often unhealthy explanations given to them by friends and relatives who are trying to be helpful. You may want to decide what you want to say to your child, and share your explanation with others who will be with your child. Rather than refuse their explanation, or confront them in any way, simply tell them that you have decided that the explanation you have chosen is best for your child right now, and that she needs to hear consistent explanations from others. Ask them to use a similar explanation in talking with your child. Most relatives and friends will respect your wishes in this regard, and be grateful for your direction. They are often uncomfortable with what to say themselves.

INTEGRATING LOSS INTO YOUR FAMILY

In some families, patterns of silence develop which become stronger and more isolating with each passing month. No one talks about the loss. No one speaks the dead child's name. Each member of the family handles the death separately from each other member. These patterns not only make the grieving more difficult, but also deprive each member of a vital source of support: the other family members.

In other families, grieving becomes so overwhelming that it overshadows all aspects of family life. The focus of the family is the dead child and the needs of the living often go unmet.

Your family is a living, breathing entity. As the parent, you must take a leadership role in ensuring that the dead child's memory is kept alive, that the loss is integrated into the family, but also that the living members receive the support, reassurance, and encouragement that each needs in order to become a healthy and fulfilled adult. Family life continues, even after the death of a child.

In addressing this you might find that it is helpful to establish some family rituals to honor and remember your dead child. You may remember her when you say grace, for example. You may keep a large picture in a central area, with a flower-filled vase beside it. You may set aside a weekly time for each member of the family to recall a special memory of the child. Such rituals serve to focus the family's grieving, and "give permission" to members to continue with their own lives on a daily basis.

It is important also to construct rituals for dealing with "special" days. Your child's birthday, date of death, Christmas, and other days may be especially hard for your family. Finding a way to remember your child's special days, and to include that child in family holidays will help everyone to recognize the importance of that child to the life of your family.

Following the suggestion of other bereaved parents, our family releases (biodegradable) balloons at "special" times. We write messages to our child on small pieces of paper, tie them to the balloons, and send them up in the sky. Other families plant a tree, light a special candle, or say a prayer. Ask your family to help you to build a ritual that is meaningful to each of you.

CHAPTER FIVE

GRANDPARENTS, SPOUSES, CHILDREN, AUNTS, UNCLES, AND SUCH

Our child's grandparents, aunts and uncles, cousins, and other family members mourn the death of our child as well. A spouse and children grieve with a pain as hard to bear as ours, and must cope with problems uniquely their own. Their relationship with our child, and with us, determines whether they will stand beside us or apart during these troubled and painful times.

There are as many patterns of extended family relationships as there are families in this world. No family is just the same as another, and how your family as a whole responds to the death of your child depends on the complex, interwoven relationships of the individual members with your child, with you, and with each other. Tragedy brings forth the best and the worst in us all, and our families are not exempt from this.

Our relationship with our parents and our siblings is as old as we are and has a significant history. If our family of origin has been close and supportive always, we will be able to count on their love and support through our tragedy. If our family of origin has many difficulties in relationships, if physical, mental, or emotional abuse, substance abuse, divorce, death, severe sibling rivalry, or real or perceived injustices created stresses that continue into adult relationships, their ability to help us and our willingness to accept their help and support may be severely compromised. Problems with in-laws may dilute our relationship with a sibling and affect our interaction at this most difficult time.

Whether we are able to feel supported by our families or not, I believe it is important to recognize that they, too, have had a loss. It is not as painful, immediate, or profound a loss as ours, but it is a loss nonetheless.

GRANDPARENTS HAVE A DOUBLE PAIN

Losing a grandchild seems to us very different from losing a child. However, there are many things that these two losses share in common, and some very important things which especially affect our parents as they struggle to understand what has happened.

Just as our child was our future, that part of us that would live on long past our own death, so our child was also the future of our parents, a vital piece of them that would remain after they were gone. Feeling closer themselves to the end of life, this future that would survive them had a strong and vital meaning. Losing a grandchild means losing a part of yourself, just as parents lose a part of themselves.

Our parents have, in all probability, experienced many more losses than we have. They may have lost their own parents, perhaps a brother or sister, perhaps a spouse, friends, and other relatives. They have faced their own mortality as well, to a much greater extent than we, because of their greater years. They may have felt prepared to accept death. Yet *this* death hits them with overwhelming force, leaving them stunned and helpless.

Many grandparents shared closely in the lives of their grandchildren, providing babysitting, day care, companionship, special treats and events, money for a new stereo, a home away from home, and, almost always, a sympathetic ear for secrets and problems.

Even if grandmother or grandfather lived far away, and saw your child only on special occasions, that child held a very special place in their heart. You need only to look around your parent's home to see the pictures, drawings, and mementos of your child all around you. Even the grandchild who visits rarely usually has some toys, a favorite cup, pacifier, book, or other belonging kept for them by grandmother and grandfather, who treasure that reminder of their beloved grandchild. There is a designated place for a grandchild to stay in almost all grandparents' homes.

Often, there is a very special bond between a child and a grandparent—an awareness of togetherness, of mutual dependence and relationship to you, a sharing of interests and abilities. Children argue with and rebel against their parents. Their grandparents are often their allies, and more often accept or condone behavior and ideas which you cannot.

Grandparents may have guilt over your child's death also, but their guilt may be different. They may feel that it is they who should have died, rather than your child. "Why am I alive," my mother often wonders, "and my grandson dead? I have lived my life, I am no longer needed, my health is failing. Why was I not taken in his place?"

Your parents love you, too. They suffer greatly with your pain. They feel helpless to shield you, to protect you, from this tragedy. Parents are supposed to help their children, to shoulder their burdens, to ease their load. Yet this is a load which can't be shouldered, can't be eased. The tears of a grandparent are both for the grandchild who has died, and for you, their child, who mourns and suffers.

SPOUSES AND CHILDREN ARE A SPECIAL LINK TO YOUR CHILD

If your child leaves behind a husband or wife and children, the relationship between you is essentially important.

Your child's spouse has become a widow or widower, long before this could even be reasonably expected and accepted. Like you, he is in shock and denial. He has many of the same symptoms of grief. He has, perhaps, looked down the vista of peaceful, productive, and happy years side by side with your child, and now finds himself alone and adrift without an anchor, a goal, or a direction. He is alone in the home he has shared with your child. There is the empty side of the bed, the closet filled with clothes, the second car in the driveway. His life, enmeshed intimately with your child's, is ripped asunder.

If there are children, he must plan for their daily care. He must provide comfort and support, and explanations. He must deal with arranging for day care, school, camp, and activities. He must make financial adjustments. His world is turned upside down, and he may be unable to cope.

Your grandchildren are probably confused, and have difficulty in grasping the enormity of what has happened to them. They may cling to their surviving parent, to you, or to another family member or friend for support. They may act as though nothing has happened, unable to begin to accept the magnitude of their loss. They may have nightmares, be unable to eat, fight with their friends, break their toys.

Your child's family is in crisis. While stunned yourself with grief, it is important to reach out to them, for the patterns you set may be vital in establishing the kind of relationship you will maintain in the future.

If you have had a close and supportive relationship with your child's family, you may find this a natural thing to do. Your daughter-in-law needs you, and you are there. You provide all the help and support you can, and it is accepted. If your relationship has not always been the best, it is important to reach out also. Differences, if possible, should be set aside for future discussion and resolution. For the first weeks and months, try to be as available and as understanding as you can.

Often, bereaved parents find that it is only with their beloved child's own children that they can feel some measure of peace and comfort. They are eager to help to maintain the memory of their child in the hearts of their grandchildren. Sometimes, a bereaved parent may want to "fill in" for their child by providing the love, material comforts, and time that the parent would have provided.

You are tied to your dead child, and, therefore, of necessity, to the past. With time, your child's spouse and children may find that they must look to the future. She may move away, begin to date, remarry, develop new friends and interests. They may seek a new father figure, lose interest in their father's memory for a time, set aside the toys he made, now outgrown, and stop talking about him.

It is important to understand that these are natural events: life does move on, even ours, much as we might like to stop living. It is natural for young people to try to adapt and to search for happiness and meaning. If you are able to accept the inevitability of these events, you will find that you will be able to establish a relationship with you child's spouse and your grandchildren which will be lasting and rewarding for all.

You will need to set some boundaries for the relationship. Will you take your grandchildren for a month each summer? Will they spend Easter with you? Will you help to provide money for college? Will you babysit? Keeping consistent in the arrangements that you make will help to ensure that they continue successfully.

BROTHERS AND SISTERS: AMBIVALENCE ON BOTH SIDES

In most instances, I believe, your sibling would like to offer you love and support in your loss. Most likely you would like to receive this love and support. If your relationship with your sibling has been a close one, you may feel comfortable in accepting this help, in leaning on your brother or sister, and in sharing your pain and hurt. It is a beautiful thing to see brothers and sisters gather around the parent who has lost a child, making loving and caring for you their first concern.

Many brothers and sisters, however, are unable to give or accept this much-needed support. A history of misunderstanding, rivalry, jealousy, and disappointment in each other sets the stage for a distancing, rather than an approaching, at the time of loss.

For your brother or sister, this distancing does not diminish the loss, but, rather, leaves him to deal with it alone. Removed from your mourning, he struggles on, often in silence, to resolve his own feelings of loss.

If your brother or sister has children, he or she may have a head and heart full of complex and conflicting emotions. Along with the grief at the loss of your child may be a deeply hidden thankfulness that it is your child, and not hers, who has died. Your loss may be threatening to him—he may worry that his children, too, might die. He may feel guilty enjoying the love of his children, knowing that you no longer have yours, or maintain defiantly that he has a "right" to be happy, no matter how you feel. She may resent the intrusion of this tragedy into her life, a tragedy in which she has had no part, and over which she has no control.

At times, it is a difficulty with your brother or sister's partner which causes the distancing. Your sister-in-law may resent the amount of time and thought your brother is giving to you, for this time is taken from her. Your brother-in-law may not feel any relationship to your child, and stand apart from the grieving and mourning process. You may feel he is "watching" you, judging your reactions to this loss, and you may be uncomfortable in his presence. She may not get along with your family as a whole, and be unable to extend much sympathy to you. These kinds of problems of necessity affect your brother or sister's ability to offer you the love and support you need.

You may find that distance between you and your brothers and sisters is necessary for a period of time. It may last months, or a few years, and then resolve itself gradually, leaving you with a relationship similar to that which you originally had. However, there are many situations where the differences that have been accentuated by the death of your child create a permanent break. It seems painful to think that at a time of such a terrible loss, you must endure yet another. If you feel comfortable in doing this, you may want to try to initiate a discussion with your sibling regarding your relationships, and the feelings you have about its disruption. It may be that he or she has had many of the same feelings, and that it is possible to re-establish your relationship to some extent.

Nieces and nephews around the age of your child who has died may be a comfort to you. You may feel that the family as a whole lives on in them. You may enjoy their presence, and the happy memories they recall. At the same time, their presence may add to your pain, reminding you that your own child is no longer a part of the family. It may comfort you to hold younger children, but it may also serve as a very physical reminder that you can no longer hold your own child. Older children may give you sympathy and support, but may remind you once again that your child will never reach their ages.

Whether you accept this loss as your whole family's, or yours only, will have a great impact on your relationships with them for a long, long time.

LOVE, ENVY, ANGER

Your relationship to your family at the time of the loss of your child, and for years to come, may be a conflicting storm of emotions. You love your family, but also envy them. You are angry, but also comforted. Your ability to hold such opposing emotions with equal strength may feel confusing, and, at times, make you wary of your own reactions.

There are times when you are especially vulnerable. Family gatherings are often very painful, especially in the first years. If your family has an annual Fourth of July Reunion, or Labor Day picnic, you may find that you both want to go and dread attending, aware that the presence of other intact families will only accentuate your loss. Some parents feel that they cannot attend such gatherings for the first years. Others are ready to face "reality" in these settings as well. Still others feel that the love and support of their family will shelter them through this experience, as it has through others since their child's death. The kind of relationships that exist between members of your family will determine how you feel about attending family gatherings. Let yourself be guided by what YOU want to do. If you feel unable to attend, a simple "I'm not ready" should be all the explanation that you need to offer.

Holidays are often difficult times as well. Perhaps the family has always come to your home for Thanksgiving, Passover, or Christmas. Or you have always gone to your sister's home. Repeating the same holidays in the same tradition is not possible for many parents. Recognizing this, your family may be able to change the tradition. Perhaps you will all go out to dinner for Thanksgiving, or drive to Uncle Joe's, who has never hosted a holiday. Making a new and different pattern is often very helpful. It recognizes that a change has taken place, an irrevocable change. But it preserves the family togetherness which is so important for support.

The milestones of a niece or nephew may also be painful. You want to share in the joy and excitement of Sally's graduation, Kim's Award Ceremony, Joanie's First Communion, Michael's Championship Meet, or

Connie's Bat Mitzvah. You love your niece or nephew and rejoice with them in their special moment. But you may find that you are afraid to go—afraid that you will be overwhelmed by tears and pain. I found that, for me, some occasions created a double concern: fear that the loss of my child would be felt more strongly at that moment, and concern for my family that my sorrow not spoil their special times. I found that I needed to skip special events for a time, and it is only now, as I approach the five-year mark, that I feel able to return once again to share in my family's special times.

Some of us have another kind of difficult time with family members, especially if we have lost an infant or young child. Our sister, or sister-in-law, with whom we are close, becomes pregnant, and delivers a much-desired and much-loved child. We want to share her joy. We want to welcome this new baby into our heart. We *do* participate and we are genuinely happy for the new parents. Yet we also know, consciously or buried deep within, that their joy accentuates what we have lost. We recall the birth of the child we have lost and his first days. We recall our own joy, and feel the terrible pain of acknowledging how very profound and irreversible our loss truly is. It seems as though our joy for them serves to validate the very depth of our own loss. A parent who has lost a newly born infant remembers that, like them, she planned to send out birth announcements, but instead wrote an obituary notice. Like them, she had a Baby's Book lovingly prepared, but hers would remain forever empty.

OUR FAMILY STILL

It is important to realize that these feelings of ambivalence, of wanting to be a part of our families and pulling away, of love and trust, and envy and anger, are all normal reactions to the loss of our child. With time, they will decrease in intensity, and you will regain the stability that you feel you have lost.

We are the parents of the dead child. Our lives are completely, irreversibly altered. Each day we are reminded in one way or another of what we have lost. Our family may love us, care for us, support us in every way possible. But their lives go on, flowing smoothly by us as we watch in tears from the shoreline.

Yet, I believe that we human beings need a sense of connectedness, a sense of being a part of something larger than ourselves. Our extended family provides this connectedness. If we are able to find, within all the confusion in our minds and hearts, a way to relate to them, we will find that, with time, this relationship will be an important source of strength.

CHAPTER SIX

SOCIAL RELATIONSHIPS

Our daily world is filled with many people apart from our families. Friends, co-workers, neighbors, fellow congregants, members of civic and community groups, teachers and other professionals, our children's friends and families, the checkout person in the grocery store, our dentist's receptionist, the postal carrier, and many others with whom we interact on a daily basis must both confront and be confronted by our loss.

People may learn that our child has died through the newspaper or an organization newsletter. Some learn it from neighbors and friends, colleagues at work, or a special prayer offered at church.

If our child has died after a lengthy illness, many people may be aware of our circumstances. We already might have experienced some of their reactions to our tragedy: love and support, avoidance, or a mixture of the two. Still, the finality of death may bring another dimension to their relationship with us.

Each person who learns about our loss experiences it in terms of their relationship with us and with our child, and in terms of their own life experiences. They are as unprepared to face this tragedy as were we, although, of course, they are removed from the center of our pain. They, too, must search for reasons, causes, someone or something to which blame can be assigned. They, too, might need to consider their conception of life and the nature of God or the Universe. But for many people whose lives touch ours, the greatest difficulty becomes "What should I do? What should I say? Should I bring it up, or just let it pass?"

There are also many people who will not hear about our loss unless we tell them. Friends from out of town, as well as some people whose lives touch ours only marginally or occasionally, may not know that we have lost a child. We must decide, ourselves, whether to tell them and what to say.

And then, too, there are the people whom we meet after our child has died. Our loss is not a part of the common experience of our relationship with them. Should we tell everyone? Just some people? How do we decide?

Close or distant relationship, new or old, we find ourselves from the first moments needing to face others with our terrible truths. We are vulnerable. They are uncomfortable. Yet it is important that we bridge this tragedy and find a way to relate to each other.

FRIENDS ARE AMBIVALENT TOO

Our friends often find themselves in a confused emotional state. As a whole, they grieve with us, support us, and stand by us. Each gives us the special gift of their relationship and caring, in ways that are unique to our friendship with them. They are "there" for us through our child's illness, death, burial, and beyond. But, being human, they too have difficulties in relating to this loss which may impact on our relationship.

Along with their love and support, which we sorely need, is an inner ambivalence. "This could happen to me," they may be thinking. "I'm glad it's not me. I don't know how I could handle it. Thank goodness that it is *not* me."

At first, this reaction infuriated me. I knew that it was on my friends' minds because hints of it would appear in their words, their voices, and their expressions. How, I thought, could they be so selfish, so cruel, at a time like this?

But there is another level at which I knew what they were thinking. This is the level of our common humanity. As human beings, we understand and empathize with each other by putting ourselves in the shoes of the other person. This is one of the special abilities humans have that is different from any other life form. We can sympathize and we can empathize. We can understand others. We know what pain feels like, and disppointment, anger, love, and joy. Our experiences may be different, yet the range of emotions is something that we all share. It is not hard for me to understand the feelings of another person. I do make mistakes, but in circumstances as clear and direct as our tragedy, it would be difficult *not* to be able to understand the emotions of others.

So I must believe that, were I in their shoes, I would have some of their feelings as well. This does not make me *like* their feelings, but it does help me to understand them.

If our friends have children of their own, one of the first decisions that must be made is: do we talk about our children, about what is going on in their lives, as we always did, Or should we not mention them? They may make this decision on their own, or they may look to us for cues.

Because we recognized that this would be a problem, my husband and I discussed with each other our feelings in this regard. We decided that our children were a part of the texture of our lives. We always shared each other's parenting joys, supported each other when our children had difficulties, and often included children in our social activities. To eliminate this dimension would alter, perhaps very negatively, our relationship with our friends. We decided that, although it would be exceedingly painful to us, we would continue to keep children a part of our relationship. I believe that this is the best, though admittedly a painful, choice.

We were not able to put this decision into effect the first months. Try as we could, tears would come at the mention of friends' children. It was, at first, impossible to listen. We controlled this as we could by simply not asking, and many of our friends, sensitive to this issue themselves, did not bring up children, focusing rather on our difficulties or generalities during our social contacts.

After several months, we became stronger, and we were able to listen a little. We indicated this to our friends clearly by asking about their children and engaging in conversation. Little by little, this part of our relationship has returned to its previous levels. I do not say that this is easy to do; still today, it often hurts terribly, especially if the child they are telling us about is of the same sex, or the same age, as the child whom we lost.

With time, we are better able to handle some of these painful situations. I am early in the fifth year of my loss. Yesterday, I met a friend for coffee. Her daughter, just graduated from high school, was going to be leaving home to begin college in a few weeks.

"I'm going to miss her terribly," my friend confided, nearly in tears, "I just don't know how I'll be able to handle the separation. I loved having her home and watching her grow. It's just going to be awful. I'm dreading it. I just don't know what to do."

The ever-familiar pain clutched at my stomach, mixed with the ever-familiar anger. "Doesn't she know what she's saying to me?" I wondered. "Does she have any idea of what this is doing to me? How *can* she?"

I knew that I could stop her, and relieve a little of my pain, with one word: my child's name. During the first years, I would have done it. I would have made her stop. I would have made her feel guilty for her thoughtlessness. With my ever-so-much greater loss, I would have dismissed her smaller one, made it unimportant in its context. The conversation would have ended, or have been refocused on the death of my child. She would have apologized for her thoughtlessness.

Instead, I stopped myself. I put my hand over the pain in my stomach to comfort myself. I took a long, deep breath. And I said, gently, "She'll come home for vacations, you know. And you can always go and visit."

It hurt to do that. Yet I think that, if we value our friendships, we must make an effort, if and when we are able, to keep them as whole and natural as possible. Let your own emotions be your guide.

ONE AT A TIME WORKS BEST AT FIRST

While most of our relationships involve face-to-face, one-on-one friendships, we all find that there are occasions where we congregate with others in large groups. Christmas parties, weddings, cocktail parties, special events of all kinds bring us together with many people simultaneously. Often we know some people well, some a little, and some not at all.

I noticed quickly after my child died that I was not able to handle being in large groups. This seems to be generally true of most bereaved parents. Large groups overwhelm us, and we may find that we are completely withdrawn and shut down, or tearful and unable to interact. Large groups call for "casual" conversation at a time when we have lost the ability to interact with pleasantries. We have nothing pleasant or casual to say. We need someone to "hang on to," and, in large groups, this is usually not possible.

We are vulnerable and, in a large group, it is difficult to control what is said and how. We do not know what people will ask us. We are fragile, our painful emotions very close to the surface.

It is better to avoid such large gatherings for a time. While I have sometimes been embarrassed about refusing, I have never encountered a hostess who did not understand my reluctance. It is important that you think first of all of your own needs—the group will go on without you for a time, and will be waiting for you when, and if, you want to rejoin it!

Although years have passed, I find that it is still very difficult for me to be in large groups, especially at parties that are relaxed and joyful occasions for everyone else. I'm still not able to be lighthearted and "happy" in that sense. Parents who are much farther along in their grief tell me that this will be possible, and I do believe them. But it is not possible now, and so I continue to choose very carefully and selectively the special events that I will attend.

We do, however, need contact with others. It is harmful to isolate yourself and remove yourself from all social contacts. You just need to be "in charge"—you pick the time, the place, the circumstances. One on one is usually best at first!

SOME PEOPLE DON'T KNOW WHAT TO SAY

Our friends and acquaintances know that we have had a terrible loss. In order to acknowledge it, they want to say something that lets you know that they understand. Most of the time, we accept their condolences and hugs gratefully if not happily. But sometimes people say things to us that drive us "up the wall."

A few selections, gleaned from my experiences and those of other bereaved parents, follow:

"I know just how you feel. I lost my grandmother six months ago. She was 96. I really miss her."

"My cousin's sister-in-law died a month ago. I went to the funeral. It was so sad. I know just how you feel."

"Losing a child is the worst thing that can ever happen to anyone. I know I could never handle that."

"I dream about something happening to Sharon. I just can't imagine how you can deal with it."

"YOU are the embodiment of my worst nightmares."

"Jason does the same things [your child did] all the time. I'm lucky nothing has happened to him."

"I know just how you feel. My dog died last year and I was really heartbroken for months."

"Cheer up. Losing an infant is not like losing an older child. You didn't have him for very long, after all."

"You can always just get pregnant again."

"You must feel so good to know she's not suffering anymore."

"God must have wanted him."

"The good always die young."

"Well, you've lost a child. Now you don't have to worry any more. Look at me, I still have to worry all the time." (The fact that you have other children to worry about doesn't matter! After all, you're "used to it" now!)

"Well, you've been through the worst there is. Now you know life will be better from here on in."

"Life has its ups and downs. Guess you just had a down!"

"I don't know what to say. I just can't imagine."

"I admire you. I could never handle a thing like that."

"I know someone whose child died from [something they think is worse than the way your child died]. You are really lucky!"

"I know [several names of people they know] who have lost a child too. They say you never get over it."

I'm sure you have your own collections that your can add to this list. It seems as though after we've lost a child, nothing should be able to hurt us anymore. But these kinds of statements still do!

Another reaction that I find difficult at times is when someone gets genuinely upset at the death of my child, and starts to cry or sob, hugging me all the while.

I know that their reaction is truly sincere, that they empathize and sympathize and want to show love and support and understanding, and that they are caring and sensitive and genuine. But what am I supposed to do? I am clinging to my own self-control by a thin thread most of the time. I don't want to cry, again, especially after the first years when crying and other expressions of grief have become more private than they might have been at first.

I find myself comforting the person, then stopping myself in confusion. *Why* am I comforting someone who is crying in my arms because *my* child has died. And yet, she (usually it is a she) so obviously is upset and needs comforting. Sometimes it's a crazy world!

Another whole category of people are those who say nothing, who do not refer to your loss at all when they see you after your child has died. This can be very confusing. You wonder if they know your child has died or not, but you can't see how they wouldn't know. You don't know whether to mention it yourself. You don't know if they are just too uncomfortable to allude to it, or if they just don't care.

I used to think they just didn't care, and become angry at their lack of feeling for my loss. Sometimes I would confront them with it. At these times, their stiffness and awkwardness would make me realize that they did know, but just didn't know what to say.

I once confronted an old friend, whom I hadn't seen since the death of my child, in the grocery store. A year and a half had gone by and I had never heard from her. We exchanged greetings and she told me about what her children were doing. She asked about my daughters. I could stand it no longer.

"You know," I said, "Daniel died a year and a half ago."

"Of course I know."

"I wasn't sure. I never heard from you."

"Of course you did!" she exclaimed self-righteously. "I sent you a sympathy card."

"You did?" I became confused. "I don't remember."

"Yes I did. I would never let something like that go. I would always do the proper thing. I sent a card. I did the proper thing. How could you think I wouldn't?"

"I'm sorry, then," I mumbled, "I got so many cards. I didn't notice. I just never heard from you. I always wondered about that."

"Well, you DID hear from me!"

I said good-bye shortly thereafter.

I don't deal well with this kind of reaction. Maybe I should. Maybe I should be more understanding. I'd rather have one of the crazy comments I listed above, than just deadness, avoidance, not meeting my eyes. To me that is the very height of insensitivity. You may find that you are kinder and more tolerant. I can't be!

On the other hand, another friend from whom I hadn't heard handled the loss differently. About a year after my son had died, she called me.

"I've been too upset and embarrassed to call," she said. "I know you must have been wondering. I just didn't think I could face you. But I want to. Would you go out to dinner with us?" "Of course," I answered. I was glad to have these friends back in our lives. I wouldn't have handled a friend's loss as she did, but I could understand and truly value her effort to reach out when she felt able. We remain good friends!

YOU WILL LOSE SOME PEOPLE YOU LIKED

Some old friendships, like that with my grocery store friend, end forever. Many of these have not been close relationships, although some have. Some people are not able to accept and deal with your loss. Some people are afraid of you.

You are a pariah in the world of parents. They might "catch" your disease, if they are near you. All bereaved parents experience this kind of reaction, sometimes from friends, sometimes from people they meet and "tell."

There are various reasons that people tend to avoid bereaved parents. Some of these are related to discomfort in talking about your loss, in not knowing what to say.

But some people seem almost afraid of being with bereaved parents. It's as though they are afraid that this painful infection will spread and engulf them. There seems to be an almost primal fear, something you can sense. These people exude terror. They shrink from your presence and avoid contact. They do not meet your eyes.

"If I don't go near it," I think they believe, "I can't get it. I can deny that it exists. I'll just blank it out." We are already hurt, grieving, and vulnerable, and this kind of reaction fills us with additional pain in a heart that we think can't take one iota more of pain.

Some losses bear additional burdens in this regard. If your child has committed suicide, you may find even other bereaved parents avoiding you. Our society tends to view a suicide as a failure—the person himself is a failure, and you, his parents, are a failure. Surely, many people feel, you have done something wrong that your child has decided to end his life. You brought this child into the world. He is *your* responsibility. If he has found his life to be unliveable, it is your fault. This attitude, this avoidance, only tends to reinforce the feelings that many parents of suicides have anyway, making recovery slower and much more difficult.

If your child has been murdered, the very horror of what has happened, the vision in people's minds of what has occurred, may cause similar avoidance. You are not held responsible here. Perhaps your child's death reminds others of how fragile and tenuous our hold on life is, and how unexpectedly, and beyond our control, lives can end.

If you have lost a child to miscarriage or stillbirth or infant death, you may find some of the same reactions, especially among your peers, the young mothers with whom you have shared pregnancy and childbirth and your child's babyhood. Again, there is the fear that their child, born or unborn, will also die. I know of one mother whose miscarriage left her unable to bear other children. After a few months, she decided to give away her selection of lovely and expensive maternity clothes. She had several friends who were her size and were expecting. Uniformly, her offer was refused. "Bad luck," friends said, "we don't want any bad luck."

If your child had died from certain causes, societal condemnation of them may create an additional burden for you. Parents of a child who had died of AIDS, alcoholism, or drug abuse may find themselves especially vulnerable because society tends to believe that these are avoidable diseases, and that the individual brought these upon herself. Your child is responsible for her own death and you, as her parents, share in this responsibility. It does not matter that there is strong evidence to the contrary. Society refuses to acknowledge the evidence and holds the victims responsible.

You may find this kind of avoidance even if your child has died of an "acceptable" illness, such as cancer. Just the word "cancer" and the images associated with it in people's minds cause them to avoid you.

You may also find that you become distant from friendships that were structured around your child. Parents with whom you attended high school football games, and the post-game parties that followed them, may fade slowly from your circle. Car-pool parents separate when their route no longer includes a stop at your house. Friends with whom you exchanged child care no longer can count on you. You no longer visit your obstetrician, though your girlfriend continues there. The Cystic Fibrosis parents' support group doesn't meet your needs anymore. Alanon seems pointless. Little League fathers meet without you now. The Sunday School doesn't call upon you for refreshments anymore, so you don't see the families there.

Being away from certain groups of people, especially in the beginning, may be helpful. You are coping with your loss and your grief, and additional painful circumstances should be avoided. Be careful of yourself—try not to place yourself in circumstances which will cause additional pain, until and unless you feel that you can handle it. There's no point in going to your child's school's award dinner, college graduation, religious school play, or swim team championship unless you truly feel that this will be a good experience for you. Acknowledge the thoughtfulness of the invitation, and regretfully decline. When you're ready, if you want, you will be able to attend.

MAKE NEW FRIENDS, KEEP SOME OLD

Though losses and changes in social relationships will occur, your need for social interaction continues, and you will find yourself both keeping friends and making new ones in the years that follow the death of your child.

Old friends are your first and best source of social support, ourside of your family. Old friends who love you will listen over and over to your stories, as you repeat them without end during the first months. Old friends will know you can handle only a funny movie, not a sad one, that you don't want to go to a restaurant your child enjoyed (or that you do), that you need to do things differently for holidays and reach out with an invitation, and that you need to cry sometimes, even in public.

I have an old friend who has a funny, but often gross, sense of humor. He has listened to my tears and stories without end for all the years since the death of my child. But, when times are at their very worst, he'll tell an off-color, ridiculous joke that will make me laugh in spite of myself through my tears. I know he offers it with caring and love, and, somehow, I can accept it in that spirit. I have another old friend who, for a year, lit candles in church in memory of my child every week. I do not share her religion or her belief system. But she knew me well enough to know that I would find much comfort in this—and I did. Another friend went out to lunch with me every week for the first six months after my child died. She knew that I needed to talk every week, and she gave me that opportunity. I know I can still call on her if I need her. Many good friends stayed in close touch with us—a call every few days let us know that they cared and were there to listen and help.

It wasn't always the friends with whom I was closest before I lost my child who reached out to me. Sometimes it was people I did not know well, but who, somehow, were able to empathize and meet me where I was at that moment. These developed into strong, new friendships that I enjoy today.

I also knew others who had lost a child. Unfortunately, there are a lot of us around. These friends were very special, not only because they understood, but also because they could lay out some of the steps that were ahead for me at a time when I could not see any way to move forward.

I found that I needed to talk with other people who had lost a child. I had, and still have today, a distrust of people who tell me how to feel and how to act, and what to do and say, who have not themselves experienced what I have experienced. It's not that I don't love them, or recognize their caring. It's just that I share with other bereaved parents a kind of knowledge and experience which cannot be fully understood, no matter how empathetic the friend.

When my child died, during the first week, someone left a card on my kitchen table. It said "Compassionate Friends—a Support Group for People Who Have Lost a Child Tragically." It gave me a name and a telephone number. I used it almost immediately. I went to my first meeting alone.

It took a great deal of courage to walk into that room, to face that harsh reality among strangers. But, for me, it was the best thing that I could have done. It has been the source of new and wonderful friendships, friendships that include our losses and yet transcend them. Friendships where it is all right to cry, and all right to laugh. Friendships where I could feel safe to explore my feelings, to express my deepest regrets and sorrows. Some of these have blossomed into very special and meaningful social relationships. Support groups such as this exist throughout the country, as do others that focus specifically on the loss that you experienced.

You will find that your relationships with others change through your loss. You will lose some friends, keep others, and add new friendships to the old. Each relationship, however, must be strong enough to hold your pain and sorrow, acknowledge your loss, and accept the person whom you have become.

MEETING NEW PEOPLE

Although I am now in my fifth year of loss, I am still sometimes apprehensive about meeting new people. How do I tell them of my loss? Do I tell them at all? I think the answer to these questions depends on two things. First of all, I think it depends on the situation. If I meet someone casually and transiently, at a party, on the beach, in a store, or at a meeting, I tend not to share this information unless it comes up in conversation. If I meet someone with whom I will have extended contact, I do. The second factor, impacting strongly on the first, is my own character and personality and needs.

If you are a person who is naturally open and sharing, you will find that you are more comfortable if people know that you have had a loss. If you tend to keep things, especially emotion-laden things, to yourself, you will be more comfortable not sharing this information.

Another consideration in your decision must be the uncertainty of the reaction of the receiver. Often, people are taken aback when you tell them you have lost a child. You make them uncomfortable. They know that you expect some kind of reaction from them, and are unprepared, especially in some circumstances, to react. At times, I have felt that telling someone I have just recently met places an unfair and inappropriate burden upon the person. However, being of the naturally sharing type, I often tell anyway. Because my loss is a part of me, I often feel that not sharing this information creates a barrier between myself and the person I'm meeting. Therefore, I have a tendency to share. However, the manner in which I do this has changed over time.

When I first lost my child, I told everybody I encountered, immediately. It didn't matter if I was never to see them again. The hotel receptionist, the supermarket checker, the waitress in the restaurant, all "had" to know. After the first six months or a year, I became more sensitive about how my information was received. This sensitivity has made me curtail who and under what circumstances I tell of my loss.

There are situations that are very difficult and can cause a panicked, fearful reaction from you as a bereaved parent. One of the hardest is when a person you've recently met asks you what she thinks is a perfectly harmless question:

"Do you have children?"

Or, worse yet:

"How many children do you have?"

Parents who have lost a child well beyond the first five years may be daunted at such questions. But they have had many, many experiences in answering them, and have usually found a way that feels right to them. Some just answer by telling about their living children, if any. Some include the information about the child that has died.

I find that I am unable to omit a mention of my child when asked about children so directly. I answer the truth: I have two daughters and I lost a son. I cannot ignore my lost child—it feels to me as though I am denying his very existence if I do not include him.

However, you may not want to deal with the inevitable questions that follow such a revelation, and the inevitable discomfort on the part of the hearer. Having shared that you have had a loss, it is sometimes hard to answer questions about the circumstances. If you find this difficult, you may prefer either to avoid the questions or to answer without including your dear child.

YOUR CHILD'S FRIENDS

Your children's friends have a special relationship with you. They may have known you for many years, and your home may be as familiar to them as their own. Like you, they are coping with a loss which has an enormous impact on their daily lives. They are often young, and inexperienced with death and grieving.

Your child's friends' grieving will depend, of course, on their age and on their understanding of death. Younger children may have difficulty imagining that your child is gone forever, for they do not grasp the permanency of death. Older children may be facing their own mortality, along with the death of your child. If your child's friends were involved in your child's illness and/or death, they may have issues that they themselves need to address. Adult friends of your child may stand near you in your grief, or take their own elsewhere, to a spouse or to other friends, for help.

Some of your child's friends may turn to you for comfort. They may want to be around you, share in your grieving, continue to be in your home. Some may want to try to comfort you, to reach out and tell you that they are still a part of your life. Some may find it all too painful and distressful, and prefer to stay away.

In the beginning, most bereaved parents find comfort in the presence of their children's friends. It seems a normal part of life with our child. If his friends are here, the newly bereaved parent reasons wishfully, then he will come back too. But as the days and weeks and months pass, you realize that your child isn't coming back, and you may find yourself ambivalent toward your child's friends.

Your children's friends keep you in touch with your child's generation. They share with you your child's "culture," and keep it a part of your life. You may feel closer to your child through these contacts. Having lost an only son, I find that I still enjoy conversations with his best friend. It keeps me in touch with what his life might have been like, now. I enjoy holding his arm, hugging him. There are no other young men my son's age in my life, and, in hugging him, I remember the feel of strong young muscles and a healthy body. His old girlfriends still grieve and remember, and I know that he will never be forgotten—he is part of their youth forever.

Because my child's good friends grieve still, I find that there is much I can share with them. There are memories we share together, and special, private memories they have about my child that I can save and treasure. Their thoughts about death and about my son's life are a comfort to me. It is good to know that he is remembered.

On the other hand, the presence of your child's friends in your life serves as a constant reminder of all that your child is missing. She would have been on that team too, you think, started at that nursery school, been a part of that graduation, maybe gotten engaged, married, been a mother. There is a sadness, a wistfulness, that accompanies these thoughts.

With time, you and your child's friends will develop a relationship which is comfortable for both of you. It may be that, slowly, you drift apart. It may be that you become a confidant, a kind of replacement for your child in her friend's life. It may be any of a wide, wide variety of possibilities. There is no "quick fix" here—only time will help you each find the way to grieve and grow.

CHAPTER SEVEN

A MEMORY ON EVERY CORNER

The memories of your dead child surround you, and you bury yourself in them at first, seeking relief. Every unwashed tee-shirt, car keys, stuffed animal, baby bottle, and old notebook are now treasures more valuable than gold or silver. They cannot be replaced, and you may lovingly hold them, crying bitter tears all the while, for the first several months. Others in your family may feel the need to do this also.

You may find that you need to wear an old jersey, a worn pair of tennis shoes, or a sweater perhaps long discarded. You may need to sleep with a doll, a special book or toy, or blanket that belonged to your child. Especially precious are things that smell like your child, for this familiar smell helps you to feel that your child is still a part of you.

Though this need may feel strange and unusual to you, it is very normal for bereaved parents. There is even a name for these things. They are called "transitional objects"—things we use to help us through the time of transition between the first agony of our loss and our later grieving.

I wore my child's tee-shirt under my clothes for at least six months after he died. I kept his room untouched, with the door closed to preserve the smell. I slept with his last picture in my hand, and, if I lost it in bed in the night, I would wake up in panic.

My daughters still often sleep in his football jerseys, and treasure any object that his hands have touched. My husband still wears my son's tie-dyed tee-shirts at times, and Grateful Dead teddy bears dance across his chest under his neat shirt and tie. I serve chips and dip in the bowl that he made, lovingly touching it with every chip. I drink coffee from his mug, and treasure his old towels.

Only you will know when you are ready to move a little apart. You will notice that you do not wear the clothes every day. You forget to take the toy to bed. At first, guilt assails you. How *can* I forget, you scold yourself. How can I forget my child?

It is not your child that you are forgetting. That will never, ever happen, of this you can be quite certain. What is happening is that you are holding your child in your mind and heart more surely and securely as the months go by. You are slowly becoming less and less dependent upon these "transitional objects." It is not a sign of loss of love. It is a sign that the transition is occurring. It is a healthy sign.

Old photographs become treasures as well, for there will never be others. Many parents find it comforting to sort through old pictures, and create an album of pictures of their child. Some create a special corner, wall, or area of the home which is dedicated to pictures and other mementos. Many other parents find that it is too difficult, too painful to look at any pictures, especially at first.

If you find that you cannot look at any pictures of your child, old videos, or family slides, it is not necessary that you make yourself do this. You can keep these forever, and turn to them when, and if, you feel ready. This may be a few months after your child has died, a few years, or never. You can find comfort in the knowledge that the pictures are there, that they exist, without ever looking at them.

I still feel unable to view my child's football videos. On occasion, not often, I look at old picture albums. They comfort me by recalling wonderful, funny, special moments. They remind me that the history of our family life includes my child. But they also bring me the pain of knowing there will be no such moments again, and that family pictures now can never include my child. Our family changes and grows with the years. My dead child is frozen in time—he smiles at me from his last fraternity picture, taken two months before his accident. His face never changes expression.

If your child was married, a parent, or involved with significant others, you may find that special belongings, pictures, clothing, and other things you hold dear may have to be shared. Remember always that those who loved your child, too, have suffered a loss; they, too, want to hold on to memories. There can be strength in sharing special things, and in knowing that someone treasures your child's things with love, as you do.

YOUR CHILD'S ROOM

For parents who lose a child who lived at home, just passing by, let alone entering, the child's room is a wrenching experience which cannot be avoided.

The unmade bed, the toys on the floor, the closet door left open with a jacket sleeve sticking out, the open schoolbook, the pushed-aside crib blanket faces us with a force and intensity which takes our breath away. Our child was *just here*, we know. How can it be that she is gone forever? That she will never pick up her notebook, close the closet door, wear the sweater, put the pajamas on, ever, ever again?

Each of us must address our child's room, sooner or later. Each of us will do it in his or her own way.

Some parents find that the only way to cope is to close the door, leaving it untouched. Some parents find that they need their child's whole room as a "transitional object"—sleep in their child's bed, look out her window, sit at her desk. Some parents find that their child's room is a private haven for tears and hurt and anger that is just their own. Others need to redo, redecorate, rearrange their child's room as soon as possible, wiping out every painful trace. Some need the door closed at times, to be in the room at others, and to replace things at still other times.

Whatever you want to do about your child's room is ALL RIGHT. If you want to keep it as it is, it's all right. If you want to change it, it's all right. If you want someone else, a friend, a family member, to do something with it, it's all right. If you want to avoid making any decisions whatsoever, avoid going in it at all, that's all right. There's no "right" or "better" way to handle this very special place in your home. The way that is most comfortable for you is the right way.

The way that is most comfortable may change with time. If you cannot deal with your child's room at first, the passage of time may gently ease the sharpness of the pain. You can always decide to open the door.

If your child was living on his own, you may be unable to postpone making some of these decisions. A rented apartment must be vacated, a home sold or rented, a dorm room emptied. You may be forced to confront your child's room before you feel ready.

There is a very special pain in the task of gathering up your child's belongings, and deciding, in those first weeks, what to bring home and keep, and what to give away. Try to make the process as comfortable for yourself as you can. Perhaps a roommate can sort and pack some things. Perhaps a friend, a sibling, or a spouse can accompany you. Perhaps you can do it all in one awful agonizing day. Don't hesitate to ask for help and support, or to accept the offers of others if you are comfortable with these.

If you feel that it is best to deal with your child's room alone, build in some support for yourself for afterward before you begin—a visit with your other children, an evening with a close friend, a walk in the woods, a funny movie, a soothing bath—you will know best what will help you. Just knowing there is a plan for "after" can help you know there *is* an "after," not just the "before" for which you still grieve so strongly.

YOUR CHILD'S BELONGINGS

Some parents need to hold on to all of their child's belongings. All of us need to hold on to some of them. Some parents need to remove some of their child's belongings from their home soon after their child has died. Sooner or later, when you are ready, you will need to make some choices and decisions.

It hurts to touch and see our child's clothing. Many things have special memories—the prom dress she wore with that cute boy, the Cub Scout uniform he was so proud of, the bathing suit from swim team, the "coming home" outfit you had imagined her wearing so many times, the school jacket you bought him his senior year, the college sweatshirt that she tore the sleeves from when it was still new, his first dress shirt from elementary school graduation, the business suit he got with his first paycheck from his first "real" job, the tee-shirt from last summer at the beach, his favorite soft blanket-sleeper— these may be things from which you can never part.

You may choose several items to use as transitional objects. Some things may be too "special" even for that—you need to preserve them untouched.

Our children also had clothing to which we may be less attached, either because the items themselves were not unique, because there are a number of them, or because they were not our child's favorites. Socks, underwear, ties, jeans, sport coats, headbands, and barettes tend to multiply in our child's drawers and closet, and we may not feel personally tied to each and every item. That coat you bought three years ago which she never wore, a tee-shirt in the "wrong" color, or a dress you never liked may have no special meaning to you. This is a good place to start sorting.

There are various choices you can make regarding the clothing that you cannot keep. You can offer it to your child's friends. You can give it to a family member. You can give it to someone you know who is in need. You can give it to charity—Goodwill, the Salvation Army, your church's clothes box, a nursing home. You can give it to a consignment shop. You can throw it away.

Don't hesitate to be creative in handling this painful task. One bereaved parent, who lost an eight-year-old, loves needlecraft. She has found a lovely pattern for a quilt, with eight squares, one for each year of her child's life. Each square will be quilted with "special" pieces of clothing from that year.

You may find that you need to go through your child's clothes and dispose of them very soon after she dies, needing to be free of these painfully simple reminders. You may need to put it off for a number of months or years. Or you may find that you do it little by little, one small step at a time, starting with the least important items.

Your child may have other belongings that were important. Special toys, boxes of CDs or tapes, a bicycle, stereo equipment, a football helmet, hockey stick, camera, golf clubs, or fishing pole all need to be kept safely, given to someone who will use and treasure them because they belonged to your child, or given to someone in need. You may find yourself holding on to every scrap of paper, every coloring, every notebook, every bank deposit receipt—everything that has your child's handwriting. Depending on your wishes, and on your storage space, you may want to hold on to these important mementos as long as possible—maybe forever!

Small items may be placed in a special "remembrance box," perhaps with a picture of your child on the top. It's perfect for jewelry and pins, a special pen or crayons, small craft items your child may have made, a cigarette lighter, keychain, favorite cup or bottle, Scout awards, and so forth.

Large items, like a car, are especially difficult. It is painful to separate from your child's car or truck, but you may find that it impossible to keep them. You may lack the space, or find that you cannot cope with the painful reminders always before you. I drove my son's car for almost a year after his death. I refused to sell it, or let anyone else have it. He had chosen it, he had driven it, it was a part of him. In time, with gentle help from my husband, I was able to let go of this very special part of my son. I needed to—driving it was too overpowering.

YOUR HOME

Our home has always been that special space in the world that was ours, that was private, that was comfortable. No matter what the circumstances under which we live, almost all of us have tried to make our home a sanctuary for ourselves and our loved ones.

Whether our child was at home with us or not, our home is full of our memories, hopes, and dreams, which always included him. It is inseparable from our images of her playing, talking on the phone, giggling and laughing, snacking and watching TV.

Without our child, our home is a strangely silent place. It looks the same. Everything may be in the same place. But, suddenly, it is alien. We look around blankly, unfamiliarly, at first, for the very air that fills the spaces in our rooms has changed. It is weighty with our sorrow and filled with our despair.

Many parents find themselves feeling very ambivalent about their home. At moments, home is where you run to be safe and alone, to cry in privacy. The very walls seem to hold you up and to offer you support in a torn-apart world. There is comfort here. There is security.

At other moments, home is a mockery of your life. There *is* no safety, no solace, anywhere. The very texture of the walls reminds you of your loss in a way that suffocates and overwhelms, and you want to be out, away, somewhere without memories. You want to run as far from home as you can, and never look back. You can't leave soon enough.

If your child has died at home, after a long illness, due to an accident, or through suicide, you may find that remaining in the home is not possible for any length of time. But even if home was the place where you received the tragic call, or the knock on the door, you may find it too painful to remain there.

Usually, though not always, it is best not to make a decision too quickly. A very rough rule of thumb suggests waiting a year before making a decision about moving from your home. It is usually best not to make decisions when you are in a state of shock, when you are unable to think clearly, and when you have not had the time to sort through your feelings. It may be that the positives outweigh the negatives, and that you decide to remain in your home. Or it may be that you need to start over in another home, with your child in your heart, but without the actual physical surroundings that overwhelm you so easily.

Moving is a major life decision. If you are alone, you need to consider carefully the effect of the move on your mental state, support system, job, and so forth. If you are living with others, it is vital to include each person in the decision-making process, and to consider the effects of the move on each. A decision made by you alone may affect other members of your family drastically. It is best to share your thoughts with them and arrive at a decision together.

YOUR NEIGHBORHOOD

Your neighborhood, community, town, or city, like your home, may be a source of support at times, and of pain at others. There is a memory of your child at every turn. The school bus he rode still passes your house. The gas station where he worked last summer still sits on its corner, three blocks away, though you may prefer not to use it. His play group still meets at the playground, and the posters for her high school bake sale are in the grocery store. You still have to pass his favorite tennis court on the way to the grocery store, or the baby furniture store where you bought her crib on your way to work.

Our neighborhoods sing a song to us. It is a song of all the familiar joys and sorrows and loves and arguments of our own and our children's lives. Sometimes, the song is a lullaby that soothes and embraces us in warmth and comfort. Sometimes, the lullaby cannot soothe us, for there is no warmth and comfort left anywhere. There is only pain. Sometimes, the song becomes a nightmare of broken dreams and betrayed hopes, the music an alien and unfamiliar and abrasive rhythm.

Our neighborhood world may be a source of strength and support, for our friends and families are there. We may lean on others who know and love us, who knew and loved our child, who stood by us and continue to stand by us. Our history is here, in the song of our neighborhood, and we may feel that we join the story of our child's loss to the neighborhood song, adding a new sad strain to the old melody.

For most of us, there is a new song that we sing, sometimes. It is our song, a song of sadness, and we must sing it alone. The people in our neighborhood world cannot always hear our song, for the music is unknown to them. It does not strike a chord anywhere. They continue to sing the old song, unaware.

But we are aware. We know that their lives continue as before, when ours have changed, and this knowledge brings pain. We see their children, our children's companions, playing. We hear their teenager's parties. We watch them pack up for a family vacation. We feel alone, apart, and may long for a place where there is no song that we used to sing. We may long for a place where, when we learn its song, our sad song of today will be a part of the harmony, if not of the melody.

Like moving from our home, leaving our community is not an easy decision, and it is best to make it slowly and thoughtfully. Some parents choose to remain in their community, either in their home or in another. Some move to a neighboring community. Some move across the country. Some are committed to jobs that keep them close by, while others decide to change jobs along with homes and communities. Only you and your family can know the best choice for you.

These decisions are difficult and painful. Give yourself and your family time to consider them, plan carefully for the choices you have made, stopping to take a deep, deep breath when you need to.

CHAPTER EIGHT

SPECIAL PROBLEMS

Each parent who has lost a child has "special" problems. Some parents have certain kinds of circumstances that have a strong impact on their grieving, and they read the previous chapters of this book through a "special" lens.

Parents who have lost a child through miscarriage, stillbirth, and infant death, parents of suicides, parents whose children died violently, parents of children for whom there is no "final resting place," parents who have lost an only child or more than one child, and single parents have unique and special concerns. A very "special" problem is that of a parent whose child is missing or kidnapped, and whose whereabouts are unknown.

Recognizing the special needs of some parents, support groups that focus on these needs can help. Talking with other parents who have experienced similar circumstances can help you feel as though you are not alone, and suggestions for dealing with your unique circumstances from those who have "been there" can be very helpful. Professional help is often needed as well.

PERINATAL DEATH

Parents who lose a child due to miscarriage or stillbirth may feel especially "cheated." Their child was born quiet and still. They have not had an opportunity to "parent" their baby, to hold, hug and kiss, or nurture. They have waited through long months of pregnancy, experienced the excitement and expectation, felt the baby's movements, heard the baby's heartbeat, and waited with a heart filled to overflowing with love to welcome their child into the world.

Parents often say they "never got to be a mother," or "didn't get to father." There is sadness but also anger and frustration. They lost a child they never knew. A mother describes her "empty arms"—arms that needed to hold and to rock, with a need as physical as her need for food and sleep.

I think it is helpful to think of "parenting" as something that begins, if not at conception, then at the moment in which a parent decides to have the child. From that moment on, the child "exists" for that parent, in a sense, and there is already love and care.

It is easy to see this love in many young expectant mothers. Smoking and drinking are immediately forgone, as are certain kinds of food. Vitamins become a daily staple, as do any prescribed medications. Rest must be considered carefully, certain kinds of activities avoided or curtailed. One young mother endured painful laboratory testing without anesthesia, for the sake of the baby. Another left the job she loved for one she liked much less, but which was less physically demanding. Another normally active and busy mother remained in bed, week after week, as ordered by her physician. Another faced monthly hospitalizations and transfusions cheerfully.

Care of your baby begins in the womb. You *are* a good mother when you obtain prenatal care, and follow a good plan of health, rest, and nutrition. Fathers show love and care as well, by shouldering some of the mother's responsibilities, ensuring rest and health, giving love and support.

The tie between a mother and her baby before birth is complete. If something goes wrong, it is difficult for the mother not to blame her body or the doctor or the hospital. After all, she did her part in taking good care of herself. It is difficult for the father not to blame as well.

"It's not FAIR!" mothers and fathers cry in their pain, "It's just not FAIR!" No, it isn't.

Parents who lose a child through miscarriage and stillbirth also bear an especially painful burden in social interactions. Attempting to comfort, friends and family, as well as acquaintances and co-workers, say things like:

"Well, it's not like losing an older child."

"You ought to be grateful. There was probably something really wrong."

"It's nature's way!"

"It can't be *too* bad. After all, you never even saw him."

"You can always just get pregnant again."

"How come you had a funeral? It wasn't even a person."

"Well, you'll get over it in a few weeks."

These comments attempt to downgrade the seriousness of the parents' loss at their own expense. They are painful and cruel and all parents who lose a child in this way experience these kinds of remarks. Though recent years have brought greatly increased understanding on the part of the general public, our society still often reflects the mistaken idea that a loss through miscarriage or at birth isn't as "real" or as "painful" as the loss of an older child.

Parents who have lost a child during pregnancy or at the time of birth often have been raised in this society. We have absorbed and internalized these very ideas about perinatal death and miscarriage into ourselves. This may cause us to believe that we don't have the "right" to grieve for our child, or ask for help and support. We may find ourselves downgrading the seriousness of the grief that we are experiencing, and shutting it within ourselves. We aren't "supposed" to grieve as long, or as hard, we believe, as parents who have lost an older child. We fight the sorrow within ourselves silently, sometimes embarrassed and ashamed of the depth of our own feelings.

I often see this at bereaved parent groups, when parents who have lost a child through perinatal death or miscarriage say things like "We're afraid of you 'big guys' [the ones with the losses of older children]." "You know so much more." "You've had so much more experience." "You've *really* been parents." "You must hurt so much more!" It's as though they believe that their pain is second-rate, less important, not as serious.

I do not believe that there are *degrees* of parental suffering. All parents suffer terribly when they lose a child. I do believe that there are different *kinds* of suffering—all are equally real, valid, and deserving of acknowledgment and support. The kind of sorrow parents experience when they lose a newborn or an unborn child is different, because the parent's experience with the child is different. It is bounded by the mother's body, the delivery room, the neonatal intensive care unit.

No one in your world but you (and your doctor and the nurses) has had any direct contact with your child. No one else has any memories of your child. You may feel that you cannot seem to make this loss "real" for anyone in the same way that loss of a child known to others is "real." And this further invalidates your pain.

Parents who lose a child later in life know something of their child's disposition, appearance, tastes, personality. They have had much experience with touching, holding, and caring for their child. Parents who lose a baby during pregnancy or at birth do not have any of this kind of knowledge and experience. They must build their own image of their child, create it out of their love and dreams and imagination.

There may be other special circumstances for you as well. Although a young mother may be told there is "nothing wrong," and that she can successfully carry another baby, doubts plague the parents. Especially if you have lost your first child, or more than one child, fears of never being able to have children may haunt you. It is helpful to discuss another pregnancy with your physician, who may be able to give you the assurance you need.

And, in some rare circumstances, this fear may be true, and parents are faced with a double tragedy: loss of a child they may never have known, and loss of an only child as well.

When you lose a baby born quiet and still, there is usually no visible sign that your baby ever existed. Far from the experience of bereaved parents who are overwhelmed with clothes and belongings, you have nothing that "smells" like your child, nothing your child has touched, and no memories of your child's smile. In place of these, you have an empty crib, neatly folded blankets and diapers, and a layette your child will never use.

A young couple made a "picture" of their baby, stillborn, using only a baby blanket, a rose, and a lock of hair the nurse had given them. You may be more fortunate than these parents and have a picture of your baby—a very special treasure.

Parents who have lost a child through miscarriage or stillbirth receive little recognition of their loss from others. They have nothing to hold onto of their child. They worry about whether they will ever be able to have a baby of their own. They have lost the present moment of joy they had expected. But, in a special way, they have also lost a part of their future, the future their baby was going to share with them. Your future was built around this baby, and you grieve for your lost dreams and hopes.

If there is no father in the picture, and you are young, your pain is just as tragic, your loss just as great. If you are newly married, the loss of a baby may place additional strains on your marriage at a time when you are still adjusting to living together. Your sexual relationship may also be affected by your loss. If you are unable to share your feelings or comfort each other, you may need to seek help.

Perinatal death support groups may be connected to hospitals or exist through separate organizations. Of course, professional help may be advisable as well.

LOSS OF A CHILD IN INFANCY

Sometimes babies die during the first year of life. Some were born with illnesses that precluded health and growth. Others die through Sudden Infant Death Syndrome, accidents, abuse and neglect, or other causes. Losing an infant is especially painful because the first year of life is one during which your baby is wholly and completely dependent upon you. If something goes wrong, it must be your fault, for your baby is much too young to be careless, foolhardy, or otherwise irresponsible herself.

Parents who lose a healthy infant are often overwhelmed with guilt.

"If only I hadn't left her with the babysitter."

"If I hadn't let him take that toy to bed with him."

"If I hadn't given him such large spoonfuls because I was late."

"If I had not gone back to work and put him in day care."

"If I had gone to check on him last night."

"If I had't trusted my boyfriend [sister, neighbor] to watch her."

"If I had gone to the doctor as soon as he got sick."

"I shouldn't have let them play in their room."

"If I had just let the phone ring while he was in his bath, or taken him with me to answer it."

It is natural that you should have these thoughts. But I believe that dwelling on them over a long period of time is not helpful nor fair to yourself. You loved your child—if you didn't, you wouldn't be reading this and you wouldn't be grieving. You did the very best job that you could in taking care of her. Think carefully of all of the loving care that you gave her, each and every day. You got up in the night, went for walks with the stroller when you were exhausted, got diapers with the money you used to use for the hairdresser, called the babysitter every two hours. You rocked her when she was sick, kissed her hurts, changed her diaper. You loved her, and she knew that you loved her. Your love was the most important thing in her life. She felt secure and comfortable and happy with you.

Unfortunately, accidents and disasters do happen, and, much more unfortunately, one did happen to your child. Grieve for him but do not erase all of the good parenting that you provided, all the love that you gave, that you still give to this child.

If you lose a baby due to an accident for which one parent was more responsible than the other, this will create a major difficulty in your marriage. Because the baby can't be held at all responsible, one of you will usually shoulder all the guilt and blame. The other partner may say nothing regarding blame during the first weeks and months. He may even help the parent who feels responsible to deal with her feelings. You may both feel that your marriage is stable and that you have weathered this tragedy well together.

After a period of time, however, he may find it impossible not to blame, thus reinforcing her own sense of guilt. He may accuse verbally, loudly and often, shouting out in his pain and anger and grief. He may be silent, showing his anger and his accusations by looks only, or in his withdrawal. The blame of the other parent, in addition to her own, may leave the parent who feels responsible unable to cope with her increased guilt. If you are having these kinds of problems, it is important to talk with your spouse as frankly as possible about your own feelings and those that are engendered by his reactions. If you are unable to work this through together so that your guilt is more bearable, marriage counseling may be helpful. It is best that both of you are involved in seeking help. If your spouse won't attend, however, it is better to go alone than not to go at all.

Some babies are born with medical problems which they are unable to survive. It is a terrible thing to watch a helpless child suffer, have pain, and die. You, the parents, may feel overwhelmed with guilt also. "How could we have made a child with such problems?" you ask yourself helplessly, knowing all the while that it was not your fault.

Parents of a sick infant may face physical, mental, and emotional exhaustion when their child dies, for the child's care may have been difficult, and knowing that the loss was imminent was agonizing. As with all losses after illness, there is also a sense of relief that the long wait is over both for them and for their baby. There may be a tinge of guilt in the relief, for life may have been unbearably hard while the baby was alive.

Parents who lose a baby due to illness may have wanted to prepare their child in some way for the death to come, to give reassurance and strength and comfort. Although such a young child cannot understand enough to be prepared, parents may still feel somehow that they did not give the baby the help he needed.

All parents who lose a baby worry over their baby's future. More than other bereaved parents, perhaps, they worry about who will "take care" of their child. Will he "grow"? Three, four, and five years after the death of your baby, and long beyond that, you may find yourself wondering how your baby looks, how he has grown, and who is watching over him. The feeling of parental responsibility, perhaps strongest during a child's babyhood and time of total helplessness, continues after death, and you will need to come to your own place of comfort and your own answers to these most painful questions.

SUICIDE

We bring a child into the world with love and joy. We nurture that child, watch over him, worry over him. We are proud of his accomplishments and empathize with his failures. We have given our child not only the best of ourselves, but of the world as we know it. Having a child is always an act of faith—faith in the possibility of a good, happy, rewarding life, a life that is worth living.

Your daughter may have given you indications of problems for many years. You may have tried every way that you knew to help her to be happy, to want to live and grow. You may have sought help from professionals and provided medications. She may have had ups and downs for many years before her crisis. She may have tried to leave home, failed, returned. She may have succeeded and be living far from you.

Your son may have always seemed to be happy-go-lucky and loved life. He may have given you no warning of problems. But a breakup with a girl, failure at school, issues of sexuality, loss of a job or position may have created a sudden and severe depression. You may have been aware that your son was depressed and unhappy or you might not have known.

You may have seen your child seem to improve. His unhappiness may have appeared to lessen, even to disappear. He may have seemed calm, even happy. You were grateful for his progress and felt hopeful that things were going to go well at last. You finally let out the breath that you had been holding and relaxed, only to find that the inner peace came from a decision made, which was later put into effect so tragically.

You may have had an argument with your child over her behavior or ideas. She may have totaled your car, gotten into trouble with the police, flunked out of college, or had another problem that seemed insurmountable to her. She may have been too afraid to tell you, yet knew that you would find out. She loved you dearly, and did not want to disappoint you.

He may have done something which, if it became public knowledge, would have been an unbearable humiliation to him. He may have embezzled funds, had an affair, used drugs. He may have feared the criticism and censure, the publicity, or a jail sentence.

There are an infinite number of reasons that our children may have decided that they did not want to continue to live. Whether you feel that you had a role in your child's decision or not, you still feel a sense of betrayal of trust, of a rejection so overwhelming that it takes your breath away.

Guilt, personal guilt, is often the first and strongest emotion for parents of suicides, often lasting for many years. After all, we reason, we are the parents. Parents are supposed to be able to "fix things" for their children. That's what being a parent is, after all—being able to protect your child, help your child, make life good for your child, give your child what she needs to be happy. We didn't, couldn't "fix things," and our child died. We have failed her, and failed as parents.

The particular circumstances of your child's death may increase your agony. He may have died without a word, or a note, leaving you feeling that he did not even want to share a last thought with you, his parent. He may have left a note filled with pain and recriminations.

She may have died far from you, or in the next room. If she died far away, you may be filled with guilt. Perhaps if you had been nearby, had gone to visit that last weekend, called that last evening, she might not have done it. If she died in the next room, you might have heard the shot. You may have been the first person on the scene and found a sight which is forever etched in your brain, etched in your child's blood.

Whether you were confronted with the death scene or can only imagine how it must have been, you wonder how he could have done it. What was he thinking of, those last minutes? How did she feel when she swallowed all those pills? How could he have held the gun to his head, or kicked the chair out from under himself? Were there any regrets? These are questions which must remain forever unanswered.

Parents of suicides feel terribly guilty and responsible no matter what the circumstances. Recriminations can fly between spouses, among family members. There is a pervasive sense of failure and of shame.

You may find that you do not receive the same kind of sympathy, understanding, and support as other bereaved parents. In some obscure way, you recognize avoidance from others, adding another, unnecessary pain to your already terrible grief. During the first months, when parents need to repeat the story of their child's death over and over, in order to understand what has happened, and, with repetition, recognize that this loss is real, parents of suicides cannot tell the story as easily, nor receive the same support. You may find that the story of your child's death horrifies others, even as it horrifies you. Others can avoid it; you cannot. The events are repeated over and over in your heart, in silence and in sorrow, as you try to work toward some kind of understanding and acceptance.

While all bereaved parents sometimes sense that others avoid them, for fear of "catching" their tragedy, parents of suicides find that this reaction is common. In addition to fear, our society as a whole does not accept suicide. We tend to consider suicides as failures, and their families also as failures. Suicide in this country tends to be condemned, and the parents are also condemned.

To add to the problem, until recently suicide was a crime for which one could be jailed in most states. I find this difficult to understand, as I have difficulty with the distinction between the physical and the mental in terms of pain. As a nation, we recognize the possibility (or at least are aware of the surrounding controversy) that one can end one's life if one is in terrible physical pain, or if one has a terminal illness. We call that "euthanasia" (euthanasia means "good death"). We do not recognize that mental pain may be as severe and as painful, that some mental conditions may be as terrible as the physical ones. We call death caused by mental pain "suicide," with all of the negativity and shame that is associated with that term.

You yourself are a part of this culture. You have absorbed its attitudes and values. You have absorbed its condemnation of suicide. Yet you must search for a way to reconcile these cultural norms with your child's action. There are support groups geared specifically to families of suicides to which you may turn for help. Others have walked the difficult road you must travel. Others will listen to your story with acceptance and offer warmth and caring.

It is difficult to reconcile with the death of your child by his own hand. It is painful to think that he was in such terrible agony that death was preferable to continuing in life. And yet, I think that, for your child, suicide was an act of strength. It was action, as opposed to passivity. Your child rose up against her pain and ended it. She is at peace, more at peace than she may ever have been. May her peace reach out and touch you, giving you comfort.

VIOLENT DEATH

Finding a measure of peace is extremely difficult if your child has died as a result of the violence of another person. In addition to bereavement, you must face the fact that your child's death was avoidable, and that someone's willful act is to blame.

Your child may have been killed quickly, shot or stabbed. Often, however, there is also the agonizing knowledge that your child was beaten, tortured, raped, or left to die slowly, and that he suffered terribly before death.

The horror of your child's death echoes in your mind day and night, without end. You may need to contact your physician to consider medication to calm you and enable you to endure the first months. You need professional help, support, and time—it takes a great deal of time to find a measure of acceptance.

You need an enormous amount of support when you have been confronted with such unbearably painful events. Like other bereaved parents, you too will need to repeat your sad story over and over, until the constant repetitions wear down your shock and horror.

While others reach out to you in sincere empathy and support, their horror at what has happened to your child often adds to your pain. You are living with this tragedy every moment of every day. It is always with you, as it is not with anyone else. You have repeated the events as you know them over and over, both to yourself and to people close to you.

But others who hear of your tragedy do not have this same sad familiarity. Their reaction is often like your first one: horror, and disbelief. Although in these sadly violent times we are confronted with crimes daily through the news media, such immediate experience as yours shocks others as a news story cannot. Their reaction may trigger a return for you to those first moments of unbearable pain. Their faces mirror your horror, validate it, and justify it.

While the validation may be a source of support, many parents find themselves helpless before the very force of others' reactions. Though you cannot shield yourself completely, you may find that providing fewer details may protect you from the most extreme reactions.

In addition to the thoughts that wear a sad circle as they travel round and round in your mind, you may have to be involved with ongoing criminal investigations and prosecutions. You may have to testify at a trial. You may be asked questions about your child which may be difficult and painful. Your anger, frustration, and pain are constantly fueled by these legal proceedings. It is as though no matter how hard you try to erase the terrible images from your mind, you are brought back to them by legal repetition and review.

If the perpetrator is not found, you may be unable to find peace, or to give up the search. You may become angry with the police investigation, and feel that not enough is being done to bring your child's killer to justice. As year follows year with no progress toward resolution, your anger continues to burn hot and hard, and your desire for rightful revenge continues just as strong as it was at first.

Courts often do not act as you believe they should, and a sense of justice may elude you even if the killer is brought to trial. After a long and agonizing rehash of your child's tragedy, the killer may be found insane, or be given a sentence not in accordance with what you feel is deserved.

One of the most difficult and painful situations occurs when you know the perpetrator personally. A parent whose child is shot by his best friend or classmate, by a lover or spouse, or by a neighbor has been betrayed by the very person she trusted with her child. Several of the most painful murders I have worked with involve such situations: a thirteen-year-old boy shot in the face by his best friend; a high school classmate shooting a friend and burying him in a shallow grave, then riding off on the dead child's bicycle; a husband strangling his wife to death in a drunken rage; a man shooting a neighboring teen to death for walking on his "property." We are confronted with such events regularly on the nightly news. But we can never, never imagine that they can happen to us!

It is important to secure legal assistance and advice for yourself, so that you may have some protection from the legal process, and so that you may be fairly represented. Parents of Murdered Children, a national self-help group, will help you to understand and untangle all of the painful and awkward legal situations you may encounter, as well as provide ongoing support.

Parents who have lost a child violently often find it very difficult to move through the grieving process. They remain "stuck" in their wholly justifiable anger, desire for revenge, and for justice. These feelings occur whether the perpetrator is known or unknown, punished or not. Their child has been violated, and, through their love of that child, they too have been violated.

Although our anger is wholly understandable, as time passes, we become more and more aware that this inexorable anger is not hurting the perpetrator. Rather, it is destroying us. If this happens, we may want, or need, to explore ways to move beyond it.

When another human being violates us, directly or through our child, we feel a strong sense of outrage—justifiably so. However, we often also feel a sense of powerlessness or of lack of control. This perpetrator has, after all, taken something of ourselves—our self-image, our faith in "man's humanity to man," our belief that if we are good people we will be treated with kindness and fairness and justice. He or she has invaded our personal space, our body, our soul, through what has been done to our child.

In a sense, we have lost a part of ourselves to the perpetrator, who has had the power to cause us this incredible pain. We mourn the loss of our child, the violation of our child, and also the loss of the wholeness of our own self. As long as the perpetrator's power over us remains, in the sense of his or her ability to hurt us, so long we will not be whole.

It is, for most of us, not possible to forgive. The injury is mortal, and there is no forgiveness possible. Yet, I do believe that we have an important task, for we have still many years to live. We must reclaim the possibility of peace for ourselves in these years to come. We must reclaim, somehow, that lost piece of ourselves. We must find the way to let go, and to let ourselves become whole once again.

We can do this only by trying (I recognize the enormous difficulty of this) to distance ourselves from the violence, by "letting it go." Something awful, beyond description, has occurred. But it is past. Our child is no longer in pain, no longer suffering. Whatever our personal beliefs about the hereafter, most of us accept that our child is at peace. It is *we* who are not at peace, and the harm that the perpetrator has done hurts only us, and not our child any longer. We must take away from him or her the ability to continue to hurt us.

Through whatever means are right for us—religion, therapy, meditation—through specific techniques such as thought-stopping or substitution, through some emotional distancing from the event, we must dissolve the perpetrator's power over us.

It is only after we have accomplished this enormous, but essential task, that we may be free to remember our child as we wish to remember him, with love, happy and whole once more.

WHEN THERE IS NO "FINAL RESTING PLACE"

Although many of us know our child is not "really" at the cemetery—at least, not the child as we knew and loved her—we may find a great deal of comfort from visiting the grave site, planting flowers, and leaving little gifts or mementos. There is a "place" for our child, a visible, tangible place where her body lies. We go to that place to be "with" her; we may talk to her, read to her, cry to her.

Some of us, however, do not have this solace. Our child's body was never recovered, or no longer existed after the accident. There is a specially painful ache in that knowledge. Sometimes, there is the additional concern that our child may have suffered before death, a suffering that, in our minds, can be drawn on and on because there is never finality, never a point of closure.

You may feel that your child is not "at peace," that he is forever in limbo, with no place to "be." This is especially hard if your child has vanished with no traces. One bereaved parent tells of the horror of knowing that her son was lost at sea, and that his body can never be found and buried. Another's son fell asleep while driving, crashed into a tree, and was burned with his car. There were no remains.

Parents whose children have died in airplane crashes are often left with no trace of their child. The parents who lost their children on the Pan Am flight over

Lockerbie, Scotland, from a terrorist bomb have found that this special pain unites them, and have formed a support group that meets annually at Syracuse University's memorial to their children on the anniversary of their death.

How you react to this additional burden is often closely related to your religious and spiritual beliefs. You may find comfort in knowing that your child is "all around you," or that "his soul is free." You may feel closer to your child because he can be "everywhere" and you do not think of him as being in a particular place.

Many Americans choose cremation after death, rather than the traditional burial, preferring the purification of fire to the natural decomposition of earthly remains. Of these, many ask that their ashes be scattered, so that there is no place anyone can think of as where they "are."

These are choices that they made, you may rightly say. But I was not given a choice. I would have chosen to bury my child. I want, I need, a place to go where I can feel that my child is nearby. I want a tombstone, a marker. I want to be buried next to her when I die. Why was I denied this small bit of comfort?

We can never know the "why" in this life, perhaps. But we *can* help ourselves and preserve the memory of our child. We can create a place where she "is."

You know the places that were special to your child. Some of these are too public or otherwise unsuitable for you. But there will always be some, if you think really hard, that are quiet, private, and easily accessible to you. Most of us find comfort in nature, and you may find that an outdoor spot somewhere special may be just right for you.

There may be a park bench where the two of you sat and talked, a quiet corner of the school playground, a place at the beach where he liked to go, a tree he could see from his window, a pond you walked around in the cold a few weeks before he died, a dead-end street where she smoked surreptitious cigarettes, a place at the zoo where the animals range freely and there are rarely other people. The possibilities are infinite.

You may want to make a list of possible places, and go to visit them. Do you feel at peace there? Do you feel the presence of your child, in spirit, or in memory? If you do, this may be the perfect place for you.

You may want this to be a special place, just for you and your child, or you may want to include his other parent, or your other children. Take your time thinking this through, for this is an important decision you are making.

When you have decided that this is the special place for you, the place to "be" with your child, you may want to bring something there—a small token of your presence, and his, in this spot. Place it carefully and realize you may have to do this many times unless there is a way to secure it. I find that burying something of my child's, or something that is beautiful, in a special spot helps me to feel his nearness. It may be something as simple as a seashell, a rock, a pine cone, a marble—something that you can connect in your mind with your child.

This is now your special place to be with your child. His body is not there, but the memories you hold are, and I believe these are more important. You will build these memories, enlarge them, each time you visit. Perhaps, someday, something very, very special in your life, or in the lives of those you love, will come to be in this very special spot. And your child's presence will be with you to share the moment.

LOSING AN ONLY CHILD

The pain of parents who lose an only child comes not only from the agony of the loss of a beloved child. It also is rooted in their very selfhood, for "parent" was a major part of how they defined themselves.

Are you still a "parent" when you lose an only child? If you feel that you are not, then a part of yourself that was vital to you is no longer there. And, along with mourning for your child, you find yourself mourning for that lost "parent" that you used to be.

Parenting seems a natural part of life, especially if you *are* one. After all, human beings are born, grow, bear children and raise them, become old, and die. That's how life is supposed to be. But your life is no longer that way. You bore a child, an only child. You had one child only, either through a carefully planned decision, or by circumstance perhaps not of your choosing. That child is dead. You will still grow old, and you will still die, but the bearing and raising of children is a part of the human experience that no longer includes you.

For all parents, from the beginning to the end of time, our children are our immortality, that part of us that will outlive us, that shares our features, our disposition, and the values and beliefs that we have worked so hard to communicate. In time, we believe, they too will have children, and so that part of us will continue to live on in another generation. Can you look at the picture of a distant ancestor, long gone, and see your own eyes, your own expression? In this same way, you know, you will live on in the eyes and expression of your children, grandchildren, and great-grandchildren.

Our role as parents forms a major part of our lives. Especially if our children are still at home, our days are filled with carpools and activities, correcting homework, preparing dinner, washing clothes, and making beds. They are also filled with setting limits, arguing over the car, teaching manners, and being a willing ear at all times and under all circumstances. Best of all, they are filled with hugs and kisses, bedtime stories, a "heart-to-heart" talk. Parents dispense love, advice, caring, and nurturing to children of any age, near or far. It is what we DO. It is who we ARE.

Our children are central to our lives, and also to our self-image. In addition, much of our social lives are structured around our children. We become friends with our children's friends and classmates. We teach Sunday School because our child attends. Football breakfasts, Parents' Weekends at college, Scouts, swim team, choral group, and basketball team—all our children's activities involve us and other parents as well, so that we build friendships that comingle with our children's. When we lose a child, we may also lose those friendships, for our child was always their reason for being. If we lose an only child, we may find that a significant part of our social interactions are affected.

For these and many other reasons, the task of parents who have lost an only child is an especially difficult one. We must grieve over our child's loss, be angry, depressed, and frustrated. But, also, we must redefine who we are. We must build a new life, new friendships, new interests and activities. In a sense, we must rebuild ourselves, and this is a major project for parents who are already vulnerable, perhaps immobilized and depressed.

Your new life need not abandon your old. In a very special sense, you are still a parent. You love your child, and treasure all of your memories and mementos. You need to integrate these into the new life that will develop, and not try to deny them. They are, and always will be, a part of who you are.

You did not become the person that you were in a day, a week, or a month. You did not become that person even in a year. It has taken a lifetime to build that person. You must be gentle with yourself as you begin to rebuild. It will take time. You may find yourself exploring paths you never knew existed, defining new goals and purposes and values. Take the time that you need, and let yourself once again *be* yourself.

In trying to understand who I am, now that I have lost a child, I have found that it is helpful to remember the person that I used to be, before I had any children. That person, that young girl, was whole too. She was OK. She had loves and hates, played and worked and laughed and sang and cried. She cared deeply for many things and, wonder of wonders, she had the same values as the person I am now. That person is still me, and I believe I can draw on her inner resources for help. Knowing that somehow gives me strength and a special perspective. Perhaps it may help you as well, as you reach back into your past to find your future.

LOSING MORE THAN ONE CHILD

"You're so lucky," people have actually said to me. "You've already lost a child. Now you don't have to worry anymore like I do." Can you believe that???

Some people really think that losing one child is the most that can happen to a parent. Some of us know differently, for we have lost more than one. Twice, three times, sometimes more, we have gone through the pain and sorrow of loss, the slow, labored steps of bereavement. It doesn't get easier with practice. If anything, it gets harder, more painful. The "why me's" are overwhelming for a parent who loses more than one child.

Each child is unique and special. Our relationship with each child has been different. And we grieve for each differently.

Some parents lose two or more children in a single incident, such as a car accident or plane crash. Such tragedies leave us unable, at first, to comprehend the enormity of our grief, and much time and effort and patience are needed even to begin to allow ourselves to understand what has happened.

Often, diseases have a genetic root, and a family may have several children carrying the same illness. One father visited his child, dying of cystic fibrosis, every lunch hour and every evening after work. He held her and loved her, brought her toys, and played games with her. He treasured every moment, for he had already lost a child to this disease and knew that this one would not be with him for long.

A bereaved parent who was the mother of two Tay-Sachs disease boys had to watch the first grow sicker and weaker by the day, until he died in her arms at three or four years of age. The second, an infant when his brother died, was also diagnosed with the disease. As symptom and problem followed the inexorable course of this tragic disease, she watched her second child grow weaker and sicker, knowing all the while the steps ahead which would lead inevitably to his death a few years later.

Another parent found herself losing baby after baby in the last months of pregnancy, due to different causes each time. Each pregnancy was filled with the terror of what could come, so that there could be no moments of joy, anticipation, and relaxation. Each time, she would grieve her lost baby, then gather her strength, and try again. It was four pregnancies later that she finally gave up, unable to stand the interminable months of waiting for the seemingly inevitable.

Mental illnesses often seem to have a familiar pattern as well, and parents may lose two or more children to suicide, substance abuse, or aggressive acting-out which so often places children at risk.

Sometimes we lose more than one child for two different reasons. One bereaved parent lost one child to leukemia and another, years later, to suicide. Another parent lost one child to cocaine addiction and a second child to an automobile accident. Still another lost one child in a plane crash and another to AIDS. The possibilities are endless.

As long as we have children, we worry that something will happen to the children we still have. This worry is different than the worry of parents who have not lost a child, for we know that this can happen, that it is real. It has happened once. It has happened twice. It can still happen again.

When a family has lost a child, I believe that the loss itself engenders special vulnerabilities that other families may not experience. The other children, grappling with loss, anger, and guilt, watching their parents mourn and grieve, tend to be more prone to depression, suicide, substance abuse, or risk-taking than the general population. Sometimes subsequent deaths seem related to previous ones in this manner. We can feel as though we are powerless to stop the cycle of grief and loss and maladaptation from continuing to its painful and tragic completion.

Each of us has lost a part of our future with the loss of one child, and a still larger part with the loss of more than one child. The pain, frustration, anger, and guilt we feel are different with the circumstances of each loss, but we must experience all of these emotions and reactions each time. Different situations, thoughts, or ideas, years after our loss, will trigger a memory, pain, or a feeling of grief for each child. Each is a life cut off, tragically, too soon.

Some of us may lose two or more children near each other in time. For others, many years separate our losses. When this occurs, we may feel guilty for not "mourning" the first child with the same intensity and immediacy as we mourn the second or third. We have distanced ourselves from this loss with the years, as we are intended to do to survive. But the newer loss brings the old one again clearly into focus. We don't have the same force of feeling, but we do feel the pain and make an undeniable association between the two. If you have had a stillbirth, for example, or lost a child in infancy, the pull of your family and your other children may have created a distance between the person you are now and your loss. You remember the baby in your thoughts, but he is not a part of the daily life of your family. When you lose another child, you remember all of the pain that you experienced with the loss of the first one.

I think it is important to let yourself feel both of your losses. You need to reclaim your first loss in order to understand better what you bring to a subsequent one. In Chapter 2, we discussed the "you" that you bring with you to the death of your child. Your "you" has your previous loss woven into the fabric of your very being.

If you did not resolve issues around the loss of your first child, or if you did not fully acknowledge the importance of that loss, this will play a very central role in your understanding of your second one. Years ago, our society discounted the loss of an unborn child, or a stillbirth, much more than it does today. You may have found little support and understanding as you tried to accept and understand your loss. This may have caused you to set the loss aside and try not to think about it at all, rather than work through some of your experiences and feelings. Years ago, there were no support groups, counseling services, or books for you to turn to, and you may have tried to help yourself all alone as best you could.

If this is your situation, both losses will need to be reconsidered as you mourn the loss of your second child. This is a different world in terms of loss and bereavement. There are many resources available to help you. You have only to reach out to them.

THE SINGLE PARENT

There are about as many reasons for single parenthood as there are single parents. Divorce, separation, death of a spouse, reasoned choice, and planned or unplanned out-of-wedlock pregnancies are some of the more common reasons, but yours may be different. Your living arrangements are just as unique. You may have married or remarried, you may be living with family, partner, or significant other, or you may be alone.

The child who has died may have been living with you, you may have been sharing the child with her other parents, or she may have been living primarily with the other parent.

Your own unique combination of circumstances will impact strongly on the way you relate to the death of your child in the context of your relationships. Because relationships also affect the person who you are individually, your special combination of beliefs, character traits, and world view will have a strong effect as well.

Chapter 3 touched on being alone with the loss of your child from the standpoint of separation after the tragedy has occurred. But, with a divorce rate hovering around 50% nationally, and a skyrocketing rate of out-of-wedlock pregnancies, many of us encountered the loss of our child as a single parent.

There are special circumstances in loss for single parents. There is no one to share the pain and the load, no matter how differently people grieve. There are feelings of guilt and blame, responsibility and anger, and a loss that may be added to an older, previous tragedy.

Single parents whose child was in their care when the death occurred face an additional burden. There is no one else with whom to share the responsibility, and no one else to miss the child in the same way that you do. There is no one to help you with the painful tasks of the funeral, the child's belongings, your home. Alone, you face your other children, your family, and your friends, with what has happened.

In many cases, you and your child alone were the family unit. Loss of your child means being all alone at home, having no one to care for, talk with, or share with. Such a loss can be especially devastating if much of your life was focused on this child, and he was your "reason for being."

If there is another parent in the picture, from whom you have separated some time ago, other issues may need to be understood. The child died "on your watch." It is easy to feel guilty and filled with blame, even if your child had a lingering terminal illness. You were taking care of her when this happened. The other parent was not.

If your child did not live with you, your feeling of loss and pain may be compounded by the knowledge that you were apart from your child, and that you were not included in her daily life. You "missed out," and your child did not reach the stage of independence, perhaps, where she might have been able to choose to relate to you on an intimate basis. You were waiting and waiting for her to "grow up," and she never will.

When there are two parents involved with a child, and the child lived with one parent, the way in which you interact with and understand each other over this tragedy and loss will likely be affected by the history of your relationship. If you were on "friendly terms," you may be able to cooperate in making arrangements, give each other some sympathy and support, and acknowledge that the loss belongs to you equally.

If, however, you were not on good terms and contacts were always filled with arguments, resentments, and a tug-of-war over the affections of your child, death will only magnify and intensify your poor relationship. Parents can be very hurtful and destructive of each other when they lose a child, and you may be extra vulnerable. It is vital to secure the support and assistance of another person in these situations. Your parent, sibling, current spouse, friends, relatives, or a counselor or therapist are all good potential sources of this kind of support. Let the person or persons know what the issues are, and, if possible, have them accompany you in circumstances where you feel there may be pain and stress.

Single parents may be more prone to depression. You may feel that you've made a "mess" of your whole life: your marriage or love relationship was not successful or abruptly terminated, and now you've lost a child. Those self-esteem issues that affect us all affect the single parent more strongly, perhaps, due to the lack of support system inherent in the situation. Severe, strong depression lasting over a period of time may make you feel prone to want to end your own life—you imagine that you will get away from your pain, be once again with your child, and possibly "revenge yourself" on those who did not give you the support you felt you needed.

All parents who are alone, away from their child's other parent when their child dies, need a great deal of support. All the pieces may already be in place in your life, and all you have to do is make a phone call or reach out. If they are not, one of the first concerns you will need to address is this one. We all need a support network to help us through these unbearably tough times. Single parents who feel alone, isolated, or abandoned need this even more.

MISSING AND KIDNAPPED CHILDREN

There is a pain that never ends, a search that lasts a lifetime, for parents whose children are missing, kidnapped, or who have disappeared in some unknown way. We search for our child on every street, on busses and subways and trains and planes, in every group of people. We think we see his back, and run to take his arm, and find the face of a stranger looking questioningly into our own. We see her dress in the distance, worn by a little girl with auburn curls instead of blonde. We travel to another country and search though unfamiliar fields and streets and villages. We watch every newscast, every special program, hoping to see that beloved face.

Perhaps we blame ourselves—for that moment of carelessness, when we looked through the clothes rack in the store, and lost our toddler; for the argument that made her run away from home, that seems so silly now; for letting him hang around with the gang.

Perhaps we blame our country: the Armed Services were supposed to protect and look after our children, not leave them alone, lost, and abandoned. Years have passed. In some cases, our children have been "declared dead," but we have no evidence. We do not believe, and we continue the search long after our government officials have abandoned it.

In many instances, we do not know what happened. Other parents can ask: did my child suffer? Was she hurt? Painful questions—for *us*, still in the present tense. Is my child hurt? Is he suffering?

And then, the questions that are special to us: how can I find him? What else can I do? Did I look everywhere I can think of? Hire enough detectives? Press the police and missing persons bureau enough? How long do I think she can be alive? How long until I give up hope?

Parents of missing children cannot have the sense of closure, however painful, that is possible for other parents who have lost children. They are never sure that their children are, indeed, dead, for there is no conclusive evidence to assure them of this painful fact. They remain in limbo, forever.

Should I accept that she must be dead? Should I give up? "Giving up," in this sense, may feel very much like a betrayal. If I give up, you think, who will care? Who will keep on looking? Yet, can I look forever? Do I have the strength? Should I keep all her schoolbooks? His clothes? His sisters are sharing a room, and they want a room of their own. Should I redecorate his, and let one of them move in?

Can I ever live again? Smile again? Have joy again? How, when my child is lost, maybe hurt, maybe suffering? Should I think of myself as a parent who has lost a child? But maybe I'm not, our minds scream back at us, maybe I'm not.

Is there a reason that you chose to read this book? Somewhere, deep in your heart, do you believe that you have lost your child forever? I believe that you need to keep your child alive in your mind and heart as long as that is possible for you, but that, when it is no longer possible, you may need to let go in some way, and grieve for your loss. It is not an abandonment, not a betrayal; it is a very real human need. We all need to move through our losses, to find a place of peace. It is impossible to maintain the same intensity of pain, of hope, forever. Sometime, the intensity must lessen, and we must rest.

Parents whose child is missing are very much at risk themselves. Their desperate search leads them to exhaustion, and to placing themselves at physical and emotional risk. The juxtaposition of constant stress, tension, fear and dread, and that bit of hope that keeps on hoping, is draining and never-ending. It is often necessary to seek professional help and support on a long-term basis, and possibly, very eventually, to seek some kind of closure and some kind of peace, while still allowing for that bit of hope to live in our hearts forever.

CHAPTER NINE

SPIRITUALITY AND RELIGION

Each of us encounters the world with a unique understanding of why and how all things came to be. Faith and religion inform many of us, helping us to see order and structure in the universe, and to find a place of hope and peace.

Each of us also encounters the world as a human being, sharing with all other human beings a common need for connection with something wider and greater than our individual selves. Together, we share a common connection with the transcendent.

Before we can begin to think about the impact of spirituality and religion on each of us as we grapple with the loss of our children, we need to establish a common language, so we can understand each other. Though I know this is a difficult task, I would like to suggest some definitions that may help.

"Spirituality" can be defined as the universal human need that strives for a connection with the transcendent, with a power beyond our individual selves. Spirituality seeks to relate our single, human being with the infinity of the universe. For those who believe that there is a Divine Power, a God, "spirituality" may include a relationship with that Being. However, it is not necessary to have a formal belief system to have "spirituality." It is something all human beings share.

"Faith" is the system of beliefs and values present within one person that relates the individual to the transcendent. Again, this may or may not include a concept of a Supreme Being.

"Religion" is a communal expression of faith, a shared system of beliefs and values, and a shared world view. Religion formalizes and structures our individual system of beliefs and gives a direction to our spirituality.

Though we all share in spirituality, most of us have also grown up with some formal system of beliefs and values—in other words, with some religion. As adults, we may have held strongly to the religion and faith in which we were raised. We may have chosen to question our earlier beliefs and altered or amended them, or changed them altogether. We may have chosen to separate from any formal system—from organized religion—and developed our own unique faith, our way of relating to the transcendent.

Whatever we believed until the death of our child, most of us found our faith and religion very shaken, at least at first. Harold Kushner's book, *When Bad Things Happen to Good People*, explains the problem very well, I think, for those parents who believe in a Supreme Being. He says many of us encounter our child's death and find that what we believe doesn't seem to fit with the loss of our child. We tend to believe that God is all good and that God is all powerful. But, if God is all good, and all powerful, how could our child have died? Why didn't God save her? Was it because God was not all good? Or not all powerful? How can we keep holding onto these two beliefs in the face of our loss? Some of us do not, and lose our faith. Some of us find a way to reconcile these beliefs, and remain faithful. And some of us who may not have been religious in a formal way before the death of our child find renewed strength and hope in religion.

"FINDING" GOD, "LOSING" FAITH

While some parents are able to continue to practice their religion, or follow their belief system, in the same way that they were doing before the death of their child, many parents find themselves swinging wildly, unanchored anywhere. We are unsure of our beliefs, question, reject, reformulate, renew. We know (perhaps) what we believe today. Tomorrow—we are unsure, and this uncertainty creates its own vulnerabilities.

Each parent deals with these issues differently, and this often places *another* load on already shaken and overburdened marriages. It is not unusual for one parent to turn fervently and sincerely to religion for help, and find solace and sustenance there, while the other refuses any help, denies belief in a God who "could let this happen," and turns away from previous beliefs and practices. Especially at first, it is very important to allow ourselves space, to give each other acceptance, wherever we are in our understanding of religion and our child's death.

Many parents are "angry at God" for "taking" their child. This anger, or blame, can manifest itself as an avoidance of religious practices and attendance at church, synagogue, or temple. You may be aware of your anger, and purposefully avoid any contact with religious institutions, or you may find yourself staying away or finding excuses, without even being fully aware of the reasons for your avoidance.

For some parents, this anger is a temporary reaction. You find that, after a time, a very little bit at a time, you are able to return to your religious practices and beliefs. For others, the break seems permanent. I say "seems" because none of us can know, in truth, what awaits us down life's road.

Some parents don't avoid contact with religious institutions, but just "do what's expected" without seeming to draw any strength or comfort from the observance or practice. Perhaps, although angry, parents may fear that their child will suffer in another world if they abandon the outer forms of their belief systems. It is better to follow ritual, parents may reason, "just in case" it's important. This kind of "bargaining" may prevent guilt, but does little to help the parent spiritually.

Other parents find themselves drawn closer to God, to religious practices and beliefs, than ever before. Something terrible has happened, they may reason. I can't do anything about it, either to help my child or to help myself. I can only "give up and leave it to God," and God will give me that help, perhaps also give my child the help. Giving up control to God can be a very comforting way to handle the turbulence of the emotions that churn within us.

Feeling that it is impossible to find a valid reason that justifies the death of a child, parents may also find comfort in knowing that there *is* a reason, God's reason—a reason that is not given to humans to know. Acceptance of such a belief can go a long way toward helping a parent come to terms with the tragedy that has occurred.

Christian parents often find an enormous source of support in Jesus. You may have always had a very clear image of Jesus and been able to turn to him for strength and support. When your child dies, you find comfort in reading and re-reading the passages in the Bible that talk about Jesus' special care and love for children. You can visualize your child, sitting right beside Jesus in heaven, being comforted, loved, and kept safe. Jesus, the ultimate, all-giving parent, has taken the care of your child in his special keeping. This is a very powerful comfort.

One bereaved parent's eighteen-month-old baby strangled himself accidentally, while she believed him to be sleeping peacefully in his crib. She was desperate in her grief, and worried about her baby. "Who will care for him?" she kept crying, "Who will care for him?" Turning quickly to the Bible, she sought out passages about Jesus and children. She read them over and over, marking them, even memorizing them.

She searched for connections between her baby and Jesus, to reassure herself that he was being specially and lovingly cared for. She realized that her child had died on Good Friday, the day of Jesus' death. This was a strong link between them. Then, she remembered that her baby had not breathed at birth, and had been resuscitated by her physician. Because of this, she had always believed that this child was a special gift that had been given to her by God. When he died, she felt that she had been given this gift, but only for a limited time. Jesus may have had a hard time parting from so wonderful an infant, she thought. He took him back because he was so very special. Once she had found these special links to Jesus, it was easy for her to imagine heaven, and Jesus on the heavenly throne, with her child beside him.

I named my child Daniel because I loved the name, but also because of the Biblical story of Daniel in the Lion's Den, which had always seemed special to me. When I lost my child, I found myself looking for a connection to him through his name. The Book of Daniel is not part of the Five Books of the Pentateuch, and I had never read it before. But soon after I lost my child, I began to read. I learned that the biblical Daniel had had ideals and visions, had prophesied, and had had a strong and wonderful spirit. I began to feel that the Daniel after whom I had named my child could be a special vehicle to help me to connect with him. I later learned about the theory that parents do not choose their child's name at random, though they may believe they do. There is a reason why each child is given a particular name. I found comfort in the belief that there had been a "special" reason why I had named my son Daniel. Perhaps it was meant to enable a connection between us that could transcend death.

Another parent finds comfort in the religious concept of a "guardian angel." Guardian angels sit on shoulders and personally watch over and protect people. The universality of this concept can be seen in the popularity of angel pins, books about angels, and pictures of angels that surround us everywhere. She believes that her beloved child has become an angel, now that she has died. Because she and her child had a very strong love for each other, she feels that her child's spirit watches over her—indeed, that her child is her guardian angel.

If we share these beliefs, these images are there to help us. It does not matter that there are so many children who have died—a Supreme Being is able to have each and every one by his side.

A very important source of help and support is located within our religious institutions. Pastoral counseling can help many bereaved parents by providing a confidential, accepting, and understanding place to go with fears, doubts, worries, and sorrows. Ministers, priests, and rabbis are usually very experienced in working with losses and in comforting the bereaved.

THE SEARCH FOR A CONNECTION

Whether we turn toward religion or away from it, all of us find the need for a connection to the transcendent much more urgent with the loss of our child.

Most of us begin the search for a connection to our child immediately after our child dies. We need to find a way to communicate, to know she is "there" in some way. Especially if we have lost a child to a painful or violent death, we need to know that our child is "all right," and we can only know that, somehow, "through" him.

We look for "signs" everywhere, but in those early months of agony, few of us are able to find what we are seeking. There is another layer of pain in this inability to "reach" our beloved child. Already overwhelmed with guilt and anger and sorrow, we wonder if we don't know *how* to reach our child—if we can't seem to do it "right," just as we somehow didn't care for our child "right."

If you cannot seem to find a way to communicate with your child, it is especially painful to speak with another bereaved parent who has been able to achieve some connection. You cannot avoid wondering what this other parent has done that you are not able to do. Why, oh why, you agonize, did she get a sign, and I didn't? Doesn't my child love me? Doesn't she want to communicate with me? Is he in pain, somehow, and unable to communicate?

I believe that each of us can find a way to the inner peace that comes from a strong connection with our dead child. But I believe that we must first be ready to receive this connection and be able to recognize its form.

In the early months of grieving, as you know, we are "shut down." This is the natural protection that our bodies and minds give us to shelter us from the unbearable pain that we experience when our child dies. Even after a period of time, we may still be grieving agonizingly hard. When we give all of our energy, all of our strength, and all of our will to the process of grieving, as we naturally must at first, we have nothing left with which to receive a connection. Only from a place where there is some peace, some acceptance, can a connection be made with the transcendent that now somehow includes your child.

I believe that this need for connection to our child is universal. However, I also know that we respond to this need differently. Some parents will yearn openly and agonizingly. They will ask for help from pastors and gurus. They will try transcendental meditation and channeling, visit psychics, or take courses in angelology. Some parents will yearn quietly and privately, never sharing this need with another person, wanting to believe this connection is possible, but afraid to believe it, too, for fear that it will not ever be possible.

It is possible. You have only to let it be.

OPENNESS, READINESS, ACCEPTANCE

In order to achieve this connection, you must reach a special mental and emotional place. Each of us travels a different road to reach that place, because each of us is a different person.

I can best describe this as a state of openness and awareness. You are aware of yourself in the world, you are aware of your surroundings, and you see them with a special clarity and brightness. You see the world sharply and clearly, but you are, at the same time, aware of the limitations of your sight. You *know* that there is a whole other way of being, know it with the same certainty and clarity with which you see the things in the world.

Because there is this sharp awareness of another, unseen kind of being, which is around and in and through everything, you recognize that the connection that you are seeking can come into your presence, into your consciousness, through *anything* around you—your mind and heart, your senses, your intuition. It can come to you in any form. It can come to you at any time. You are open, aware, and ready.

It may not come to you quickly. But it will come—and you will recognize the connection with your child instantly!

I remember clearly the moment that I became aware and open. Like many of us, I realized that I could find a measure of the peace and harmony and beauty I needed so desperately first of all in nature. I could somehow "ground" myself in the openness of the outdoors. For me, I decided, the path to connection had to come from thinking about the oneness of the universe—a oneness that could hold both my child and others who had died before him, and myself and my living family and friends.

Even before the death of my child, I had always responded strongly to the beauty of nature. I used to wonder if the colors of the earth—blues and browns and greens—were especially pleasing to us as human beings because that was the way it was meant to be, or if they were just there, and familiar, and so we liked them. I used to enjoy exploring shades of colors—how many shades of green do you know?

It seemed natural to turn to nature after my child died. There seemed to be something about trees and earth and sky and water that held meaning. After a time, I realized that the meaning that they held was in their connection to eternity. Everything came to be, lived, and died. Nature returned to itself, and then the cycle would begin again, and out of the deadness new life would come. I remember realizing that the physicists were right—nothing could be created or destroyed.

I came to believe that the eternal part of us, what I call our souls, could also neither be created nor destroyed, for they belonged to that wholeness of nature. They were a part of everything and everything was a part of them. I was a part of eternity in the same way that my child was; in the same way that these trees, these birds, these squirrels, and these old logs were. And I opened my eyes wide and was ready to see.

Your experience may be completely different from mine. You may find yourself reaching this state in a moment of prayer or in communion with God, in a moment of meditation, in looking around the dinner table at your loved ones, in listening to music, or in any one of a million ways and places.

But, when you reach this state, you will know it.

THE MOMENT WILL SURELY COME

When you are open, ready, and aware, you have only to wait for the connection that you are seeking, for it certainly will come.

Butterflies are a special symbol for bereaved parents. We think of our child, released from the bonds of earthly life, becoming free and beautiful as the butterfly. Some of us find a connection to our child through a special moment during which, all of a sudden, a butterfly appeared, as from nowhere, to share with us its beauty and fragility. Though butterflies were not usually a way in which I connected to my child, on a least one occasion they were. I was on top of a hill, looking down on the special blueness of the Aegean Sea, in a ruined temple of antiquity. The sun was shining and I was wishing my child with me with all my strength. I could seem to feel his presence, and the joy that he would have in this beautiful place. I looked down and saw on a small bush one small, perfect, yellow butterfly. He would send a yellow one—he knew that was my favorite color. He had always given me yellow things.

We often sense a connection to our child in a rainbow. Seeing a rainbow at a special moment seems to bring us closer to her. We are at one end of the rainbow. She is at the other.

Angels are also often special to bereaved parents. We often like to imagine that our child is an angel in heaven, and look for angel pictures, pins, ceramic statues, Christmas ornaments that "look" like our child. Sometimes we seem to feel clearly our child's connection to the little figure in our hand.

These are some common symbols. But the ones that may hold special meaning for you are probably connected in some way to your own child especially. One of these, for me, is the number 32. I know it's the number of many famous athletes, but, no matter, it is special to me because it was my son's football number. He loved it so much he had it engraved on his retainer, much to his dentist's amusement. It seems to me that the number 32 appears with incredible frequency in my life at special moments.

My daughters, my husband, and I went for a little boat trip on Lake Tahoe on the *MS Dixie*, a sternwheel paddleboat that offers scenic tours of the lake. Before we embarked, a photographer took our picture, standing behind a sign bearing the name of the boat. It was a bad moment for me, for I remembered so very strongly that, years before, our family had gone on a trip on the *Mississippi Queen*. We were all excited over our first boat trip, and, as we embarked, they took our picture, one just like the one the photographer took on the *Dixie*. During the entire two hours of the cruise, I thought of Daniel and grieved. The beauty of the lake surrounded me with peace, but my heart was with my dead child. I wished he was with us with all my heart. Life had been wonderful then. It never would be so wonderful now that he was gone.

As we left the boat, the photographer called all the passengers to look at the pictures. One hundred photographs were placed neatly in pockets with numbers, so that they could be easily located by the photographer. One hundred photographs in neat rows. Our family picture appeared through the plastic pocket bearing the number 32.

Another special moment of connection with my son came with the birth of my first grandson, born seven months after his death. All during my daughter's pregnancy I had prayed. "Please, please, send me a sign," I had begged him, "let me know that you have a connection to this baby. Let me know that there is a before and after."

Worried that he would send a sign and that I would not recognize it, in the last weeks I changed my refrain. "Please, send me a sign that's so clear I can't miss it. I'm so afraid I will miss it. You have to make it really obvious," I pleaded.

I told no one of my prayer. I was so afraid that it would not come true! But, when my son-in-law came to get me at the airport, he was excited.

"Guess what?" he said. "The baby has a little red heart right on the middle of his forehead! It's a little birthmark in the shape of a heart. It's really cute!"

My son had heard me. He had sent me a sign. He didn't want his nephew growing up with a red heart on his forehead, so it faded after a month or so. But I have pictures!

These are some very obvious signs of connection that came to me. There have been many, many more. And many bereaved parents have similar stories—stories of "knowing," beyond a doubt, that their child was all right. Sometimes these come in dreams. Sometimes you may feel a physical presence—a touch on your cheek or on your hand. Sometimes you will smell the special scent of your child in the air. Sometimes it is a sign that you, and you only, will recognize.

YOUR PATH TO CONNECTION IS YOUR OWN—AND IT IS THE RIGHT ONE

I can share with you only my experience. Your own may be very, very different. You may find meaning and connection anywhere around you. Only you can know the path to choose.

Most of the time, the moment of connection will be a private one—you alone will be aware of it. Although I have shared with you several obvious, concrete experiences, most of mine, also, have been private and special only to me. No one else knows of them, unless I have voluntarily shared them.

The path you travel will become clear to you with time. It is your own path. It is the right one for you. No one else had the same relationship with your child that you had, and no one else can walk on your path. Though at times this may seem lonely, remember always that your child is there, beside you in spirit, waiting for you to be ready to reach out to her.

If your path leads toward, with, and through God, you will never be alone, for there will always be a presence beside you as you reach out toward the unknown, the place of your child. It is a place familiar to God, and God will lead you to it surely, with compassion, and with love. If you choose the path of religion, there may be guideposts along the way that will help you. You will find them in your faith, and be united with your child through that faith.

If your path draws you toward a connection with spirituality directly, you will feel the strength and power of the connection with transcendence. You will shape the course of your path to your own beliefs and experiences, and find within it all of the beauty and fullness of this uniquely human experience.

One of my favorite philosophers, Soren Kierkegaard, writes that the important moment is not choosing between the right and wrong way. We can, after all, make mistakes, being human. The important moment is the moment in which we accept the personal responsibility and choice of *being a chooser* of the path. Only you can make the decision to be a chooser. The path that you choose will always, of necessity, be the right one for you.

CHAPTER TEN

TAKING IN,
MOVING THROUGH

As I begin this final chapter, the muted voice of the television in the next room repeats and updates the news of the tragic crash of TWA's Flight 800, bound for Paris, with 229 aboard. My whole heart and soul are with the families and friends of the passengers.

There has been an interview with the principal of a Pennsylvania High School. Sixteen students and their chaperones from the school's French Club, bound for a language-immersion experience in Paris, were aboard the flight. The parents traveled by bus, in the middle of the night, toward the horror that awaited them at Moriches Inlet off Long Island.

Their shock, their disbelief and agony, and the televised images of the body bags that await them pulls at me, bringing back the unbelievable agony of the first days after the death of my child. I see the torn pieces of aircraft, pulled from the water, one at a time, and I feel as though my whole self, body and mind and heart, has been torn in pieces just as that airplane has been. I can feel the violence of the ripping-apart, the wetness of the bleeding, of those first moments and hours and days of loss. I can sense the enormous, dark pit opening for them, the chasm between past and future—a past, filled with life and memories; a future, unimaginable and unknown.

My heart goes out to them in the fullness of empathy and sympathy. Time has stopped for them, for now. I know the road that they must travel, for I have been there too.

Yet I also know with certainty that I am no longer there, in that place where time stops. I am in the fifth year of that unimaginable and unknown future, and I know that time would not stop, and did not stop, though I wanted it to so very much. I know where I am now.

Time has passed and life has continued inexorably, and I have memories now, new ones—memories of life after the loss of my child. Some are sad, bitter, and angry. But some are good also. They stand as a buffer between the person I am now and the person who first encountered the death of my child. I know that these newest brothers and sisters of ours in bereavement, too, will stand where I am, some day in the distance, in a place beyond their imagining.

THE YEARS AHEAD

You, too, have memories. Slowly, day after day, they are building. You are building too. You are building the new person you are becoming—a person quite different from the laughing, joyful one that you were, perhaps. A stronger, wiser, sadder person, but also one who has grown in empathy, love, and understanding.

In the beginning, the shock and numbness of grief shuts out all consideration of ourselves. Then comes the agony of desperate grief, of the "if only's" of guilt and of blame. We miss our child with all of our strength.

But at some point we become aware that we are grieving not only for our child, but for ourselves as well. Our child has died, but so, in a sense, have we. So has our life as we knew it. Carefully, over the years, we worked and planned to build the kind of life we wanted. We may have achieved some measure of success with our efforts. Now, we have lost it all. Where do we go from here?

From the time that my children were small, I had often read to them a poem I have always loved, by Rudyard Kipling. It seemed to me among the best advice I could offer them. I include it here, because it still serves me as an inspiration. (Patience, feminists—he was from another time!)

IF

If you can keep your head when all about you
 Are losing theirs and blaming it on you,
If you can trust yourself when all men doubt you,
 But make allowance for their doubting too;
If you can wait and not be tired by waiting,
 Or being lied about, don't deal in lies,
Or, being hated don't give way to hating,
 And yet don't look too good, nor talk too wise:
If you can dream—and not make dreams your master;
 If you can think—and not make thoughts your aim;
If you can meet with Triumph and Disaster
 And treat those two impostors just the same;

If you can bear to hear the truth you've spoken
    Twisted by knaves to make a trap for fools,
Or watch the things you gave your life to, broken,
    And stoop and build 'em up with worn-out tools:
If you can make one heap of all your winnings
    And risk it on one turn of pitch-and-toss,
And lose, and start again at your beginnings
    And never breathe a word about your loss;
If you can force your heart and nerve and sinew
    To serve your turn long after they are gone,
And so hold on when there is nothing in you
    Except the Will which says to them "Hold on."
If you can talk with crowds and keep your virtue
    Or walk with kings—nor lose the common touch,
If neither foes nor loving friends can hurt you,
    If all men count with you, but none too much;
If you can fill the unforgiving minute
    With sixty seconds' worth of distance run,
Yours is the Earth and everything that's in it,
    And—which is more—you'll be a Man, my son!

(From *Rudyard Kipling's Verse, Definitive Edition,* Doubleday, 1940)

Rudyard Kipling wrote this poem to his beloved son, and read it to him often, trying to teach him the values that it supports. When the son was sixteen, England went to war, and he wanted to join the Army. Being under age, he needed his father's consent. Despite his reservations and concerns, Kipling granted him permission and signed the necessary papers. His son died in that war.

Advice for children, yes. But advice for us too, I believe.

Yes, we have lost, and we must start all over again. Yes, we are weary, and in pain, and our tools are not only worn out, but heavy too. Yes, we know we used to have a will, but we're not sure where it might have gone. We seem to lack motivation to do anything.

And yet, we are here. We are alive. We have no choice but to go on.

Little by little, in small, hardly noticeable steps, we begin to change. Little by little, we are carried forward in spite of ourselves.

Imagine life as a strong stream, moving forward with willfulness and power. We rode that stream for many, many years. Some of us rode it wildly, recklessly. Others rode it pensively and quietly. Still others rode it carefully and cautiously. However you rode this stream of life, it nourished you and held you above the currents and ripples and eddies, most of the time.

When our child dies, a Force from somewhere seems to lift us up and toss us out of the stream, onto the dry, desert land along the shore. We sit there and weep, like the Biblical exiles by the waters of Babylon, for we, too, are exiles. We are exiles from the stream, watching wistfully and mournfully as Life flows by us.

We must sit on the dry bank to recover. But slowly, we must move closer to the stream. We must dip a finger in the water, then a hand. We bring the water to our mouths and find that it can still nourish us. Slowly, carefully, hesitantly, we must re-enter the stream, for, if we do not, we will die on the arid desert banks.

Somewhere during the first five years, we become aware, once more, of our need for the water of Life to nourish us. We begin to believe, almost against our will, often with much guilt, that perhaps we may still return to it.

We cannot return to it as the people we were before our child died. But the people we are now can and will.

Some of us are just watching the stream. Others have tasted its water once again and found it sweet. Others have waded in, perhaps to their knees.

That is the task of the years ahead. To return to the stream of Life as the person you are now, a person who has known death, loss, and sorrow. A person who understands sadness, but also values joy.

A PLACE FOR MEMORIES

You cannot move forward without making some kind of peace with what has happened. We all yearn for some measure of peace, while at the same time, we hug the pain and sorrow to ourselves with all our strength. It is all that we have left of our child, we sometimes feel. If we give it up it means our child is gone. It means we didn't care enough. It means we are forgetting.

We are so very afraid of forgetting. All too brief, or layered year upon year, our memories are our treasures. I find that every so often I must "test" myself by making myself "hear" my child's voice in my head. Can I still hear how he sounded? I recall images I do not have in photographs. I recall incidents and conversations. I worry that if I don't do this regularly, I will find that I no longer can.

We all know how memories can fade. We can't remember every detail of past events such as graduations, trips and outings, or meetings. We can't remember clothes we wore, even the names of old acquaintances. We also know our memory is not as good as it was before the death of our child.

How can we ensure that our memories of our child will remain fresh and vibrant and special forever?

I am sure that we will not forget our children. In working with parents who have lost a child forty or fifty years previously, I find that they are still able to recall small, intimate details of their child's life, likes and dislikes, friends and activities. Remember, what we may lose as we get older is our *recent* memory. Distant memories stay with us the longest, for they are embedded the deepest in our brains. Even so, we worry.

There are several things that you can do to ensure that you have preserved the memories of your child. The very act of doing these things can in itself be a part of your process of growth and change. You can write or record your memories of your child, and ask others to do the same. You can make a "remembrance box," special photo albums, collections of favorite things and writings. You can make a collage of his cards and letters, or mount photographs in pretty frames.

Use your own interests and creativity to make things that hold special meaning. In an earlier chapter, I mentioned the mother who is making a quilt with her child's favorite clothing, a square for each year. She used her love of needlework to create a special way to preserve some of her favorite memories.

Another mother made a beautiful photo album. She covered it with a tiny-flowered fabric in her child's favorite colors, and left an oval in the middle for her daughter's picture. She trimmed it with lace, and embroidered her name under the picture.

Another parent took a small old trunk and refinished it in a colorful bright blue. He painted a train, blocks, a teddy bear, and a ball on the lid. He added a beautiful, shiny brass latch. Special toys, a blanket, and his child's teddy are carefully resting within.

A parent carefully sorted through all the photographs of his child, and assembled a collection that was especially meaningful. She placed the pictures in a layout that was pleasing to her, and had it matted and framed with a beautiful gold frame.

I specially preserved scraps of my child's writing. I treasure lists he made of his favorite foods when I went grocery shopping, poems he wrote, lists of chores completed, essays for a school assignment. I got a handsome wooden box, had his name engraved on a brass plaque on the lid, and placed in it all these scraps loosely, as I had found them. I don't think my messy child would have wanted his papers neatly organized! I was preserving not only the papers, some of them crumpled and torn at the edges, but also the memory of his clutter.

Many children, of all ages, have special collections. Each item in the collection has a special memory. You remember when your child got the item, remember her holding it, perhaps playing with it, making a place for the collection in her room. If the collection is something that can be preserved (of a reasonable size, not alive, etc.), a whole host of memories can be saved with it.

My child collected decks of playing cards. He had hundreds and hundreds of them. There were subcollections: airline playing cards, view playing cards, unusually shaped playing cards, playing cards in beautiful boxes, and so on. He had built special strips along the wall of his room to mount them. I was unable to keep them in their original place. But I have saved them in a drawer and plan to get a small trunk for them. Each deck has memories of vacations, special events, and shopping trips. Each reminds me of a moment in his life—an age, an expression, a smile.

Many of our children loved music and had a large selection of CDs or tapes. You can sort through these, and choose the ones that you know were special to your child. You can place these in a special CD or tape carrier, with your child's name on it. Not only will you have something special of hers to look at, but you can also play your child's favorite songs whenever you wish. If your child loved some particular songs, you can create a tape of all of them together. You can even take this with you easily wherever you go, make copies for loved ones, or for his friends, if you wish.

If you have lost a child through stillbirth or miscarriage, or in the first few days of life, you may have few, or none, of these mementos of your child. I have seen parents address this painful problem in a specially creative way. They made a beautiful photo album of themselves, in various stages of pregnancy. Any other information, such as prenatal records, a sonogram photo, a nonstress test strip, a name band from the hospital, was added. If there was a birth certificate, this was placed in the album as well. The album was decorated in baby designs. If they were fortunate and had a picture, this, of course, took the place of honor. Sometimes, they made a card with the child's name in beautiful calligraphy.

Another parent, a photography buff, had a huge collection of still photos and videos of his child. He spent many evenings reminiscing and composing a special video, with titles, segments of film, and still photos. It was a work of art—a tribute of love from a father. Like the other memories we preserve, each was not only a picture—it was a moment in time. The father could recall taking the pictures, and viewing them with the family on special occasions. He could remember how his child was embarrassed by one photo, laughed at another, couldn't believe she had ever had hair that looked like that in another, and had gotten starry-eyed remembering her prom dress. He remembered that she had had to ask him to buy it because it was expensive and over-budget for her mother.

A parent who likes to write may find that journaling memories is a good way to preserve special moments. You may just want to start writing at random, as you remember things, sorting out the recollections later, if at all. You may prefer to organize your memories by year, or by theme, such as home, school, family parties, trips, and so forth. Develop whatever method will help the writing to be meaningful to you and will trigger the most cherished memories.

The process of preserving these memories is in itself part of our grieving. You may find it too painful to do this at first. It may take several years before you can look at some of your child's special things. As I mentioned in an earlier chapter, I have still not been able to look at my son's football videos.

Reviewing, recollecting, sorting, organizing, ensuring preservation—all of these activities help us to relive and re-experience our time as a parent to this child. The process may take a long time, and you may find yourself adding to your memory journal or photo album for months, perhaps even for years.

We need the time, and we need the re-living, for it is only in this process of going back over the events of our child's life that we can begin to lay them to rest, to reach a kind of closure. Not the closure of forgetting, but the healthy closure of a time, and an experience, that is a part of you forever, although no more chapters can be written and no more photographs taken.

MEMORIALS AND REMEMBRANCES

Preserving your memories is a special way to memorialize your child. However, some parents find that they have a need to have something outside of themselves and their child's belongings that attests to their child's existence and time in the world.

There is, first of all, the matter of the cemetery. We may have had the difficult task of arranging for a burial plot for our child. Almost immediately, or months or years later, we will want to have a stone memorial erected.

For many of us, designing a stone for our child is the last act that we can do that seems to be for the child directly. It is an important step. You will be seeing the stone for many, many years to come, and I think that it is essential that you allow yourself the time to design and create something which has meaning for both you and your child. Monument companies can be of great assistance to you. They have books and albums of designs, choices of stone and lettering, and suggestions that may help you to focus on what you would like to do.

Don't be afraid to be creative, if it is permissible in your cemetery. Children's stones often have designs that are appropriate to the child's age and interests. Parents whose child loved fish, for example, have incorporated designs of fish into their child's stone. Others designed flowers into their daughter's stone. You may want a favorite saying, such as a line from a song or a poem. You may want to include an especially meaningful passage from the Bible. You may prefer to write your own personal message and have it engraved on the stone. One parent chose to have her child's signature included.

Bereaved parents have very individual needs when it comes to the cemetery. Culture and traditions play a very strong role in our approach to the cemetery. Mourning habits and cemetery visitation differ from one culture or ethnic group to another. Some cultures and religions have carefully observed rituals and customs regarding cemetery visitation, and these can be both a source of comfort for you and a structure to follow for support.

Parents' personal reactions to cemetery visitation vary a great deal as well. Some parents find it a comfort, others a painful obligation. Still others find it impossible to visit at all. You may find this a perfect spot to commune with your child, or to reminisce quietly and privately. You may find that a visit churns up so much confusion and pain that you are unable to feel any closeness. You may feel that your child is not there, at the cemetery, and so there is no sense in visiting. It does not mean that you do not love your child.

You need to feel free to follow your own needs and beliefs, for this is always the best and most comforting way. Don't listen to advice or suggestions in this regard. Do whatever YOU need to do. You will meet many other bereaved parents, but you will find that each of you has a different approach to cemetery visitation.

There are other memorials possible for you as well. Some of these may be especially comforting and meaningful to you.

You may learn that a special fund has been created in memory of your child by friends and relatives. Or you may find that you can set aside some funds, and want to create something special that will serve as a memorial to your child.

You may want to create a scholarship fund, for example, in your child's name at her school. It can be awarded for need or merit, of course, but also for something that was special to your child. Scholarships for excellence in your child's chosen major or specialization (if in college), in your child's favorite sport, in music for someone who plays the same instrument, or in service to the community are examples of the kinds of scholarships you can create. You can send a needy child, selected yearly by the school, to camp. Your child's school will be delighted to support you in creating this memorial.

Planting trees is another meaningful way to memorialize your child. You can plant a tree at your home, in your child's "special place," at your child's school, or elsewhere in the community. Some towns and cities have special programs where you can plant a tree in memory of a person, and the town places a plaque beside it bearing the name and birth and death dates. Many Jews plant trees in Israel in memory of loved ones, and you may have an entire grove planted in a memorial forest there in memory of your child. Compassionate Friends groups have created groves in their communities to memorialize children, and there may be annual memorial services at the grove where you may especially memorialize your child.

You may choose to dedicate a garden bench in a park. Towns and cities often have park areas with benches that bear the name of the person being memorialized. You may prefer to create a quiet corner in your child's school playground, or on the grounds of the place where he worked. A sculpture, plants, or a water fountain may add something special to a place your child enjoyed.

Doing something for others, or creating special events, might be something appropriate for you. You may want to donate a selection of children's books to your library, or a corner where mothers who have lost a very young child can find books that will inform and comfort them. You can provide food at a soup kitchen every year on your child's birthday. You may choose a piece of equipment, or a plaque, at your child's place of work. You may provide sponsorship for a Boy Scout Troop. We created a special spring day at our child's religious school during which the students "skipped school" for a few hours, had a picnic, and played outdoor games—something our son might have enjoyed as a student there. You may sponsor a coffee and dessert hour after church each year on your child's birthday. Whatever you choose to do, there are always willing and sympathetic people to help you with your plans.

As with the memorial stone, it is best to take your time and think about the kind of memorial your child would have enjoyed. One parent donated a special display at the Aquarium her child enjoyed visiting. Another parent sponsored an event at her daughter's sorority. A mother who lost a young child sponsors a special event at her son's day care center every year. Our child loved sports, and we used the fund created at his high school in his memory to purchase a much-needed state-of-the-art scoreboard. It bears his name, and each afternoon, sports teams laugh and play and work under his memorial. Sometimes, I drive by and watch them, and it comforts me.

Planning for these remembrances and memorials, like preserving the special memories that we have of our child, can help us to grow and gain some measure of peace. They all help to ease our worry that our child will not be remembered. They give us comfort, while also giving something to others from our child.

SPECIAL OCCASIONS

Special occasions are stumbling blocks for all of us. They remind us painfully of the absence of our child. Yet they appear regularly and inexorably, and, in one way or another, we must deal with them.

The year that I lost my child, I dreaded the approach of his birthday, the day of his accident, and the day of his death. I did not think that I would be able to live through them.

I began worrying weeks and weeks ahead of time. I could feel the knot in my stomach tighten. I could feel the terror in my soul as I realized that I could not "skip" those terrible days. As the first of them, his birthday, approached, I developed severe headaches, nausea, and fear. I had no idea how to help myself.

At a Compassionate Friends/Bereaved Parents USA meeting, I asked for help and suggestions and took comfort in the strength and understanding and help that came my way so quickly.

"Plant a tree."

"Light a candle."

"Read a prayer."

"Send up a balloon."

"Get some pretty flowers."

The message was clear. Do not struggle through this day. Mark it, recognize it. Plan for it carefully, so that you are not left floating with no structure to support you.

We decided that we would send up balloons. Careful of the environment, I located a shop that sold biodegradable balloons days ahead of time. We decided to make a balloon ritual for ourselves. We would tie messages under the balloons for our child. We would sing him "Happy Birthday." We would release the balloons.

That first time, the frost sparkled and crunched beneath our feet as we walked out into the cold, bright, windless morning. We sang Happy Birthday, and, one by one, released six balloons. I had gotten my son a pink heart-shaped balloon that said "I love you." I watched that balloon go up—and then get stuck in my neighbor's tree.

"Nothing goes right for me anymore," I said to myself, "Even my balloon can't get to him."

Too upset to go to work, I lay down on my bed, finally crying myself to sleep. Somehow, my child seemed to come to me, and I could hear and see him as he thanked me for his special birthday present. His eyes sparkled, and he was smiling.

I told him about the balloon that was stuck in the tree. "Don't worry," he said, "I'll get the wind!"

As he said that, I could feel the cool rush of the wind against my body, pressing against me on its way out of the window. I looked up through the roof, and saw my son catching the special I Love You balloon, now free from the tree. He gathered all of the balloons and then they, and he, seemed to rise up in the sky and disappear.

After a while, I woke up, disappointed with the thought that I must have had a dream, although its clarity and force made me wonder. Stuck balloon or unstuck balloon, I knew I had to go to work. Wearily, I got ready and went outside. I looked up in the tree where my balloon had been stuck.

It was gone.

I share this special story with you because it seems to say so much: the beauty and the power of ritual, and faith, and possibilities of connection— gifts from beyond us. Every birthday, since then, we have had our balloon birthday party.

On the anniversary of his death, we try to have a family reunion every year at the cemetery. My husband and I always get there for that day, but my daughters, across the country, sometimes make it and sometimes do not. We read to him from the biblical Book of Daniel, and sing some songs to him. We bring flowers.

It is very important to have rituals for special occasions. You can have a special prayer said. You can visit the cemetery, bring balloons, and tie them to the gravestone. You can go to a special religious service. You can light a memorial candle. You can plant a tree in your garden each year. For these special days, you may want to develop a ritual that will remain as special years from now as it is today.

Your child's birthday and the anniversary of his death may be the hardest days for you, but holiday time is very difficult also. Thanksgiving, Christmas, Easter, Passover, the Fourth of July, family reunion days—all of these days that were once a time of joy and of family togetherness are now a time of renewed sadness, a time when the loss of your child is especially painful.

You may find that it helps to change the way you do things. If you always had the family for Passover Seder, go instead to the home of someone with whom you never shared the holiday. If you always went to Aunt Anna's for Christmas, consider inviting her family to your home, or going away for the holiday, or having dinner out. If you always had a picnic on the Fourth of July, choose that time for your vacation.

These changes in your customs will help you, especially at first. If, after a few years, you are comfortable returning to the old ways, do so. If not, stick with the new.

Some parents find that it is too painful to acknowledge the holidays in any way, and try to treat the holiday like any other day. Or they may stay at home, holding tightly to their pain and sorrow. Being with family or friends as usual may bring the absence of your child from the familiar group too sharply and painfully into focus.

Only you can know what is the best way to handle these special times. Think about them and make plans, just as you did for your child's birthday and anniversary. Don't let the day catch you unprepared—it's harder for most parents that way.

There are other special occasions that may be especially hard for you as well. Many bereaved parents cannot handle being in large groups of people for weeks, months, or years after the loss of their child. It's easy to avoid cocktail parties—the effort of trying to have "cocktail party talk" would be too hard for many of us anyway—but some other special occasions are more difficult to stay away from.

What do you do about your cousin's wedding, your niece's Bat Mitzvah or First Communion, your best friend's fortieth birthday party, or your boss' annual employee appreciation luncheon?

You do what you feel is best for you. You must be protective of yourself, first of all, for you have had a severe shock and loss, and know how weak and disoriented it has left you. You need to consider the occasion well ahead of time, and decide what you can do. Can you attend the wedding ceremony and skip the reception? Go to the whole thing? Stay home? Can you take your best friend out for lunch, just the two of you, instead of going to her party? Or can you just "stop by," having told her ahead of time that you are not able to stay? Can you explain to your boss that you can't attend the luncheon this year, but perhaps write her a nice note saying that you appreciate her understanding and support?

Each situation is different. And your feelings about attending will be different not only with the occasion, but also with the place you are in your grieving, and what else is going on in your life at that moment. You will need to consider each situation separately. Don't bother to try to be "consistent" or "fair." Just do what you think will be best for you. Others will understand.

I thought at first that I would never go to another gathering again, for the rest of my life. Just the thought of all those cheerful people made me cringe inside my pain. And yet, I have done it this past year, on a very few occasions and for fairly brief periods of time. I know now that I may be able to do it again—sometime.

A PLACE FOR YOUR CHILD IN PRESENT AND FUTURE

Your child is a vital part of your past. You need to find a way to make her a part of your present and of your future. You may need to find a way of keeping her a part of your family's life. It is this sense of finding a continuity that makes us, finally, able to re-enter the stream.

You may want to keep your child a part of your daily life by setting aside a special time for her. You can mention her in your prayers. You can set some minutes aside when you first wake up, or before you go to sleep, to think of her. You can remember special moments every day as you drive to work. You can look at her picture each day, even if only for a moment. You can say her name each day, even if only to yourself. You can wear a piece of her jewelry that will remind you of her whenever you look at your finger. There are a thousand ways that we can keep our child a part of us each day.

You may find that this is not comfortable for you. It may be too difficult to make a routine of any kind and stick to it. You may find that the repetition of the same thing, day in and day out, loses its meaning. You may prefer to just "spend time" with your child whenever you feel the need—sometimes just a moment, sometimes an afternoon.

One of the problems with trying to make a routine is that, should you forget, or should the pressures of your day make it impossible to follow your ritual, you may feel guilty. If you find this happening to you, you will need to re-think the special things that you are doing. They may not be a comfortable part of your lifestyle or routine.

Be careful not to force participation by the other parent or by siblings. Remember, we each grieve in our own way, and their way will necessarily be different from yours. If they are comfortable with what you have chosen to do, or want to make a ritual with you, by all means let them. But be sensitive to their needs as well as your own. They may prefer to think of your child in their own way.

The special time that you plan may seem to work well at first. As months and years go by, you may find that it no longer seems to meet your need. Be flexible. There's no rule saying you must keep to your plan throughout your life. Don't feel locked in. You have grown and changed, and the way you preserve your child in your heart and life has also changed. You may want to do something different to "stay in touch." Understand that you may feel more comfortable with an "as needed" special time, as the years go by, than with a daily ritual. This does not mean that you are forgetting him.

You have found a way to preserve memories. You have found a way to make your child a part of special occasions. You have reached out to your loved ones and tried to comfort them, or at least to understand them. You have connected with your child spiritually, through religion, through nature, through intuition, or through a path that only you and your child can know. You have kept your child a part of your life. You have found that you can live day by day, and the sharpness of the pain has blunted a little bit. It still comes back sometimes, but you know now that it can get better.

It has been a long, slow, painful road, one that you didn't ever want to walk. But you have found that there have been moments of beauty and sweetness mixed in with the sorrow.

FIRST SMILE, THEN LAUGH

The first time I smiled, I had to force my muscles into position on my face. They hadn't been stretched that way in so long, it seemed as though they had lost their ability to do so. It was a forced, fake smile. I felt that it was the polite thing to do. After all, sometimes you need to respond pleasantly to something or someone.

The second time, it was easier, though I still felt I was obligated to smile. It wasn't "natural." I smiled with my mouth, but my eyes were still blank, I knew.

As the months stretched out, through and past the first anniversary of my child's death, the smiles came without thinking, sometimes, though still not often.

What did I have to smile at?

The antics of a puppy. A toddler playing with bubbles. Lovers looking into each others' eyes. A joke. A funny movie. A smile from a friend. People smiled at me, I found myself noticing, and automatically, with the ingrained habit of years, I found myself smiling back.

I lifted my face up to the sun on the first really warm day of spring. I smiled. My husband got me a silly gift. I smiled. I looked at a funny picture of my child. I smiled.

No.

Stop.

How COULD I?

Guilt swept over me. How could I possibly smile, when my child was dead? What could there possibly be in the world to smile about? I was betraying him. I was forgetting him.

Guilt, guilt, guilt.

And yet, I had always been a happy person. Smiles came easily to me, all day long. Was it going to be possible to never smile again?

I tried not to. And failed. And forgave myself for failing.

I don't think we can grieve every minute of every day, forever. I think that we can let the sunshine in, in spite of our grief. It doesn't mean we didn't love our child. It just means that there is still life, and the possibility of joy, in us.

And then, one day, I startled myself with my laugh. The sound was half-forgotten, yet familiar. I panicked. Fortunately, I was with another bereaved parent, years beyond me in her grieving. We looked at each other in surprise, and laughed at my laugh, because we both knew, beyond a shadow of a doubt, exactly what I was thinking in that moment.

I was horror-struck.

"Do you really think," my friend said, "your son would have wanted you to be sad all the time? You know he wouldn't. He would want you to be the mother he knew and loved. And that mother smiled and laughed. She could feel joy and happiness."

Do we think our children would want us to suffer, to grieve, forever? I don't think so. I think they would want us to be happy.

I think they would encourage us to be happy. Not forget them, but then, with their wisdom, far beyond our own, they would know that we would never forget them.

YOUR CHILD FOREVER

We do not forget our children. Our bond with them never changes. But how we understand that bond does change. And we change too. Inevitably, inexorably, the death of our child changes us.

We are sadder, but we are wiser. And we also have a new understanding of ourselves. We have met with unbearable pain, and we have survived. We have strength, not the rigid strength of steel, but flexible strength. We bend, we twist and turn, but we do not break. We are made of stuff most people don't know even exists. We hope that they will never need to know. But we have turned that knowledge into strength.

We have a greater understanding of the connections between everything and everyone in the Universe and beyond. We know that we are connected to our child. We also know that we are connected to every living thing, to God, to the air we breathe and the earth we walk upon. Without all there is, we could not ourselves be.

We worry more, probably, about our loved ones than we did before our child died. We *know* terrible things can happen, more than most people do. But we also know that we individual human beings have very little control over what happens, or what will happen. We know that we must take what life brings to us and find a way to survive—no, more than that—to thrive, in spite of, or through, it all.

We are more willing to take chances with trying new things, with learning new skills or ideas. We reach out to the world and embrace its richness, knowing that, in a special way, our child is a part of that richness and feels our embrace. We learn and grow with, and through, and for, our beloved child. She would be proud of us.

We have not forgotten or laid aside our child, or our loss. Rather, we have taken it *into* ourselves and made it an integral part of who and what we are. The person we were has changed and shifted to accommodate this new, sad part of us. The shift has enabled growth and change, for it created spaces within us, spaces to grow, spaces for a new kind of love and joy and compassion.

Our children are our children forever. It is we who have changed, not they.

Before my son died, I cried in agony for him, for the life and the future that he would be losing forever. But I remember that I also said, "I've always been the mother of three. How can it be, how can it happen, that I will be the mother of two?"

And a wise social worker held my hand and said, "You will always be the mother of three, in a very special, unique way. You will always be the mother of three."

She was right. I am, still, the mother of three. Just as you are, still, the mother or father of six or four or three or two or one. What we were, we were meant to be forever. If nothing is created nor destroyed, neither is our relationship with our child, and our love for our child, and our role as parent to that child, ever destroyed.

It has taken a different form, this is true. But our child is our child, forever.

WHERE TO FIND HELP

THERAPY FOR YOU AND YOUR FAMILY

• Psychiatrists, Psychologists, Social Workers, Counselors

Getting help is a very personal thing and should be undertaken with care. Effective help requires that a good relationship be established between you and your therapist. What makes a therapist "good" for you, in addition to the proper education and skills, is that indefinable something between you that makes the relationship a safe and healthy place to explore, work through, and grow through loss and grieving.

Therapists work with individuals, couples, and family groups to provide help and support, encourage growth and self-exploration, and assist you with the very real problems that you are experiencing within yourself, in your relationship with your family members, and in your social and community life.

Recommendations are often good places to start looking for your therapist. Friends, others who have lost a child, your pastor, minister, priest, or rabbi, and your physician are usually good resources for names of potential therapists. Develop a list and then consider the objective qualities that are important for you. You may wish to find a therapist who has him/herself lost a child, one of your gender, one of your religion or race or ethnic group, one whose hours and location are convenient to you, one whose education and training inspire trust, and so forth. Screen your list with these objective qualities in mind.

You can also get the names of professionals in your area from professional associations. The National Association of Social Workers, American Psychological Association, American Psychiatric Association, and the American Association for Counseling and Development all maintain lists of members who practice in your area and may be consulted for names. Membership in these organizations requires certain professional standards which can assure you of competent services.

Your health provider may cover some or all services of a licensed therapist. There may be specific criteria regarding length of service, preapproval, and the kind of therapeutic services covered. HMOs and other managed care organizations may request that you use one of their approved providers of mental health services. It is best to clarify your insurance status prior to beginning with a therapist.

After you have compiled a list of therapists, make an appointment with the therapist who, from what you have heard, you believe you will work with best. During your visit, explore the subjective qualities that are important to you, the ones that will enable you to establish a good working relationship. Think about your decision for a few days: it's a big one. If you decide that this therapist is right for you, make another appointment and begin to work. If you have some misgivings, call another therapist on your list.

• Pastoral Counseling

All religions have rituals and ceremonies to honor the dead and comfort the bereaved. Whether it is a special mass, a lit candle, or a prayer for the dead, your faith is there to offer spiritual help and guidance through this most difficult passage.

Your pastor, minister, priest, or rabbi is also available to provide counseling, offer support, and assist you to find the help that you need. He or she has had training in working with loss, grief, and bereavement; knows you, your family, and your child; and can work with you in a familiar and comfortable place.

Pastoral counselors not related to a specific church or synagogue are also available through pastoral counseling services. You may prefer to use these services if you desire a spiritual and religious dimension to therapy, and are unaffiliated, or if you feel that the relative anonymity that can be maintained through a pastoral counseling service will better meet your personal needs.

• Group Therapy

There may be bereavement groups available in your area that can assist and support you as well. These can provide contact with others who have experienced loss, education which will help you to understand what is happening to you, and ongoing opportunities to share your experiences, a vital part of the process of grieving. Bereavement groups are led by a professional, and generally meet in public places or organizational offices on a regular basis.

You may prefer to work with a group, rather than have individual or family therapy. You may feel that both can be helpful to you in addressing the terrible loss you have experienced.

Some groups have open-door policies—that is, you can join them at any time. Within such groups, you will find people at different stages of grieving and coping. You will be welcomed and supported by others who have "been there." During the time that you remain with the group, some members will leave, and some others will join. Each person is able to attend the group as needed.

Other groups are called "closed." These meet for a specific number of sessions. Often, you will meet individually with the group leader before the group session, so that you will have an opportunity to share your personal problems and concerns on an individual level first. All members will begin together on the first session, and are expected to remain with the group through the planned number of sessions. No one may join the group after the first session, and the group develops relationships and themes from within. Such groups have clear beginnings, middles, and endings, and there may be a structure which involves different subjects during different sessions. Some groups also focus on specific kinds of losses, such as perinatal death, suicide, or death from a specific disease.

Bereavement groups may be located through your local hospital, which may also sponsor such groups. Hospice organizations often have bereavement groups, some of which are for hospice families and some of which are open to the community. Professionals in private practice may also have bereavement groups as an area of specialization. Groups are usually free of charge, or available at nominal cost.

• Support Groups

Support groups differ from group therapy in that they are peer groups which do not have professional leadership. Support groups are made up of people who have shared a common experience, such as the loss of a child, and who come together to provide support and comfort, share experiences and problems, and serve as a resource for information. Peer support groups have been found to be extremely effective in providing help to people who have experienced many different kinds of problems. One of the oldest examples of peer support groups is Alcoholics Anonymous. There are peer support groups for a wide variety of problems from overeating to gambling, drug use, child abuse, widowhood, divorce, and many other losses.

Parents who have lost a child have established a number of such peer support groups. Your area may have several of these available and you may attend one or all of them. Some parents find a support group helpful on a regular basis. Some attend during times of special pain or difficulty. Some attend several groups, drawing help and comfort from each. Support groups are flexible and accept any parent who wishes to attend.

It is not necessary that you be an active participant to attend a support group and to receive help from it. You may want to share your story, ask advice, express your feelings, or discuss a problem. You may just want to listen. Whether you just listen or share, cry or laugh, sit quietly, or reach out to others, you will find that you will both give and receive.

Many parents who turned to support groups when they lost a child have found them to be an ongoing source of strength, and continue to attend long after the immediate, shattering pain of loss has softened. Many find that they are able to assist other parents facing newer losses. Whether you lost your child yesterday or thirty years ago, peer support groups may be able to provide the caring and understanding that you need.

There are two national organizations for parents who have lost a child which have local peer support groups in most areas of the United States. These are Bereaved Parents USA and Compassionate Friends. There are also peer support groups for parents who have lost children under special circumstances, such as Parents of Murdered Children, National Sudden Infant Death Syndrome Alliance, and Survivors of Suicide.

Your local hospital and hospice organization is a good source of information about support groups, as is your social services network.

NATIONAL ORGANIZATIONS PROVIDING INFORMATION AND SERVICES

The list below includes national organizations which provide services to parents who have lost a child. Some of these focus specifically on bereaved parents, others on special problems, such as suicides, murders, or infant deaths, while others address losses in general. In addition to these, there are regional organizations in many areas of the country that can assist bereaved parents through workshops and seminars, group therapy and support groups, referrals for individual, couple, or family therapy, and other resources.

A Place to Remember
deRuyter Nelson Publications, Inc.
1885 University Avenue, Suite 110
St. Paul, MN 55104
Special resources for infant death, books and special remembrances to help parents and family members.

American Association of Suicidology
4201 Connecticut Avenue N.W., Suite 310
Washington DC 20008
Maintains a national directory of suicide survivor support groups, and a referral service for callers. Holds an annual "Healing After Suicide" conference and has a newsletter for survivors of suicide.

Bereaved Parents USA
P.O. Box 95
Park Forest, IL 60466
(708) 748-7672
Bereaved Parents USA provides a network of peer support groups, local and national newsletters, resources, and special help for parents who have lost a child and bereaved siblings.

Center for Sibling Loss
The Southern School
1456 West Montrose
Chicago, IL 60613
(773) 274-4600
Provides services, information, resources, and support for bereaved siblings.

Compassionate Friends
P.O. Box 3696
Oak Brook, IL 60522-3696
(312) 990-0010
A self-help organization for parents, grandparents, and siblings. CF has a very extensive network of local support groups offering programs, resources, and library. Most CF groups meet monthly and have telephone support as well. The organization also offers a quarterly national newsletter, a quarterly sibling newsletter, books to order, and yearly national and regional conferences.

Centering Corporation
1531 North Saddle Creek Road
Omaha, NE 68104-5064
(402) 553-1200
Centering Corporation maintains a list of resources and books which are available through them.

Grief Recovery Institute Foundation
8306 Wilshire Blvd. Suite 21A
Beverly Hills, CA 90211
(800) 334-7606
Supports Help Line (see below). There are no fees charged for time spent. The organization is centered on the principles in the Grief Recovery Handbook (see book list, below). The Institute has a network of certified people who are trained who run grief seminars and workshops all around the country. Seminars and Certification training are organized and run by the Institute.

Grief Recovery Help Line
(800) 445-4808
A public service of the Grief Recovery Institute Foundation, the hotline is free of charge and provides personal help with loss and grief of all kinds, including divorce and pets.

Hope for the Bereaved, Inc.
4500 Onondaga Street
Syracuse, NY 13219
(315) 475-4673
Carries books and resources on bereavement for adults and children, including information on how to form support groups. Also has support groups in the central New York State area.

National Catholic Ministry to the Bereaved (NCMB)
606 Middle Avenue
Elyria, OH 44035
(216) 323-6262
NCMB maintains a list of recommended resources and has a newsletter, Journey.

National Directory of Bereavement Support Groups and Services
P.O. Box 75115
Forest Hills, NY 11375
(718) 657-1277
Published and updated regularly, the directory provides a listing of support groups and services nationally, regionally, and locally to assist persons experiencing loss to find resources in their communities to meet their specific needs. There is a small fee for the directory, which is available by mail. It may also be available through your local library.

National Hospice Organization
1901 North Moore Street, Suite 901
Alexandria VA 22209
(703) 243-5900
Hospices provide individual help as well as group therapy to the bereaved. Most local hospice organizations also have extensive resources in terms of books and information for the bereaved of all ages and circumstances.

National Sudden Infant Death Syndrome Alliance
1314 Bedford Ave., Suite 210
Baltimore, MD 21208
(800) 221-SIDS
(410) 653-8226
A national organization with a system of local support groups for parents who have lost a child through crib death. They will also provide information about SIDS.

Parents of Murdered Children, Inc.
100 E. 8th Street
Cincinnati, Ohio 45202
(513) 721-5683
The national organization has a network of local support groups for parents and families. They also have a traveling Murder Wall, which carries tributes to murdered loved ones; SOS, which helps families who feel that they still have unresolved legal issues; and Parole Block, which helps to keep murderers in prison.

Rainbow Connection
477 Hannah Branch Road
Burnsville, NC 28714
(704) 675-5909
"Helping people grow through loss, grief, and change." Maintains a list of books and resources which can be ordered through Rainbow Connection.

SHARE
Pregnancy and Infant Loss Support, Inc.
St. Joseph's Health Center
300 First Capitol Drive
St. Charles, MO 63301
(800) 821-6819

SHARE assists in the establishment of community support groups for parents whose baby has died due to miscarriage, ectopic pregnancy, stillbirth, or newborn death. Maintains educational materials and resources and provides referrals to local groups.

BOOKS AND ARTICLES

The following list of books and articles have been found to be especially helpful by the members of the Anne Arundel County (MD) chapter of Compassionate Friends/Bereaved Parents USA. It is not meant to be an exclusive or comprehensive list, or to espouse a particular viewpoint or theory about life and death. These are just our favorites! We share it with you with love.

Anderson, George, *We Don't Die*, New York: Berkeley Books, 1989.

Anderson, George, *We Are Not Forgotten*, New York: Berkeley Books, 1992.

Bereavement, A Magazine of Hope and Healing, Bereavement Publishing, 350 Gradle Drive, Carmel, IN 46032, nine issues yearly.

Berezin, Nancy, *After A Loss in Pregnancy*, New York: Simon and Schuster, 1982.

Bramblett, John, *When Goodby is Forever: Learning to Live Again After the Loss of A Child*, New York: Valentine Books, 1991.

Brooks, Ann, *Grieving Time: A Year's Account of Recovery From Loss*, New York: Dial, 1985.

Cook, Alician Skinner, and Dworkin, Daniel, *Helping the Bereaved: Therapeutic Intervention for Children, Adolescents, and Adults*, New York: Basic Books, 1992.

Davis, Deborah, *Empty Cradle, Broken Heart*, Golden, CO: Fulcrum, 1991.

Eadie, Betty J. *Embraced by the Light*, New York: Bantam Books, 1994.

Finkbeiner, Ann K. *After the Death of a Child*, New York: Free Press, 1996.

Fitzgerald, Helen, *Grieving Child: A Parent's Guide*, Hamden, CT: Fireside, 1992.

Fox, Sandra, *Good Grief: Helping Groups of Children When a Friend Dies*, New England Association for the Education of Young Children, 1988.

Grollman, Eric, *Talking About Death: A Dialogue Between Parent and Child*, Boston: Beacon Press, 1976.

Grollman, Eric, *Explaining Death to Children*, Boston: Beacon, 1967.

Grollman, Eric, *Living When A Loved One Has Died*, Boston: Beacon, 1977.

Hewett, John, *After Suicide*, Louisville, KY: Westminster Press, 1980.

Knapp, John, *Beyond Endurance: When A Child Dies*, New York: Schocken Books, 1986.

Kübler-Ross, Elisabeth, *On Children and Death*, New York: Collier, 1983.

Kübler-Ross, Elisabeth, *On Death and Dying*, New York: Simon and Schuster, 1970.

Kushner, Harold, *When Bad Things Happen to Good People*, New York: Schocken, 1989.

LaTour, Kathy, *For Those Who Live: Helping Children Cope with the Loss of a Brother or Sister*, Omaha, NE: Centering Corporation, 1991.

Levine, Stephen, *Healing Into Life and Death*, New York: Anchor Press, 1987.

Limbo, Ron, and Wheeler, Sara, *When A Baby Dies*, Resolve Through Sharing, 1986.

Livingston, Gordon, *Only Spring: On Mourning the Death of My Son*, San Francisco: Harper, 1995.

Lord, Janice Harris, *No Time for Goodbys: Coping with Grief, Anger and Injustice after a Tragic Death*, Ventura, CA: Pathfinder, 1987.

Martin, Joel, and Romanowski, Patricia, *Our Children Forever*, New York: Berkeley, 1994.

Moody, Raymond, *Life After Life*, New York: Bantam, 1976.

Moody, Raymond, *The Light Beyond*, New York: Bantam, 1989.

Moore, Thomas, *Care of the Soul*, New York: Harper Perennial, 1994.

Morgan, Earnest, *Dealing Creatively with Death*, Burnsville, NC: Celo, 1988.

Morse, Melvin, *Closer to the Light*, New York: Ivy Books, 1990.

National Directory of Bereavement Support Groups and Services, Forest Hills, NY: ADM Publishing, 1995.

Park, Barbara, *Mick Harte Was Here*, New York: Alfred Knopf, 1995.

Peck, Scott, *The Road Less Traveled*, New York: Simon and Schuster, Inc., 1978.

Rothman, Juliet, *Saying Goodby to Daniel*, New York: Continuum, 1995.

Schiff, Harriet Sarnoff, *The Bereaved Parent*, New York: Penguin Books, 1977.
Schiff, Harriet Sarnoff, *Living Through Mourning*, New York: Penguin Books, 1986.
Smedes, Louis B., *The Art of Forgiving,* Nashville, TN: Moorings (Random House), 1996.
Swain, Jasper, *On the Death of My Son*, Northhamptonshire, England: Aquarian Press, 1989.
Stevens, Velma, *Grief Work*, Nashville, TN: Broadman Press, 1990.
Tengbom, Mildred, *Helping the Bereaved Parent*, St. Louis: Concordia, 1981.
Ulene, Art, *How to Survive the Death of a Loved One*, New York: Random House, 1987.
Veninga, Robert L., *A Gift of Hope: How We Survive Tragedies*, New York: Ballentine Books, 1985.
Williams, John, and Cherry, Frank, *The Grief Recovery Handbook*, New York: Harper Perennial, 1988.
Wolfert, Alan D., *A Child's View of Grief*, Fort Collins, CO: Center for Loss and Transition, 1991.

• For Children and Adolescents

Buscaglia, Leo, *The Fall of Freddie the Leaf*, Thorofare, NJ: Slack, Inc., 1982.
Grollman, Eric, *Straight Talk About Death for Teenagers: How to Cope with Losing Someone You Love*, Boston: Beacon, 1993.
Grootman, Marilyn E., *When a Friend Dies: A Book for Teens About Grieving and Healing*, Minneapolis: Free Spirit, 1994.
Mellonie, Bryan, and Ingpen, Robert, *Lifetimes*, New York: Bantam Books, 1989.
Nystrom, Carolyn, *Emma Says Goodby*, Elgin, IL: Lion Publishing, 1990.
Powell, E. Sandy, *Geranium Morning*, Minneapolis: Carol Rhoda Books, 1990.
Rothman, Juliet, *A Birthday Present for Daniel: A Child's Story of Loss*, Amherst, NY: Prometheus Books, 1996.
Tems, Roberta, *The Empty Place*, Far Hills, NJ: Small Horizons Press, 1992.